Common
BIRDS
of
Alberta

J. Duane Sept

Calypso Publishing

First printing, 2004

National Library of Canada Cataloguing in Publication

Sept, J. Duane, 1950-
    Common birds of Alberta / J. Duane Sept.

Includes bibliographical references and index.
ISBN 0-9730390-5-1

    1. Birds--Alberta. I. Title.

QL685.5.A86S46 2004   598'.097123   C2004-901596-6

Front cover photo: Long-eared owl by J. Duane Sept.
Back cover photos: Canvasback, ring-necked pheasant and birdwatchers by
    J. Duane Sept.
Printed in Canada by Ray Hignell Services Inc., Winnipeg MB.

Published by:
Calypso Publishing
P.O. Box 1141
Sechelt, BC Canada
V0N 3A0

www.calypso-publishing.com

Table of Contents

Quick Photo Guide to the Bird Groups

Loons   p. 11

Grebes   p. 11

Pelicans   p. 13

Cormorants   p. 14

Herons   p. 15

Swans   p. 15

Geese   p. 16

Ducks   p. 17

Osprey & Eagles p. 25

Hawks & Allies   p. 26

Grouse & Allies p. 31

Turkeys   p. 34

Rails & Coots   p. 36

Cranes   p. 37

Sandpipers & Allies p. 37

Gulls   p. 42

Terns   p. 44

Pigeons & Doves   p. 45

Owls   p. 46

Nighthawks   p. 51

Hummingbirds   p. 51

Kingfishers   p. 53

Woodpeckers   p. 53

Perching Birds   p. 56

Welcome to Birding

The pursuit of observing birds has become one of the fastest growing recreational activities in North America, from a casual and occasional pastime to an intense passion. Birding can be enjoyed in urban and rural settings and at any time of year—spring, summer, fall and winter. Some birders have life lists and many participate in Christmas bird counts as well as breeding bird surveys. Still others plan their vacations around good birding locations.

The sights and sounds of our winged wonders bring pleasure to all, young and old, and a great deal of interesting information has been discovered about our birds and their behaviors. This book will help all birders to understand the magnificent free-flyers of the area.

How to Use This Book

The birds in this book are arranged in order of evolutionary sequence, the method that is used in most bird references. This order is quickly learned and makes it easier for the novice to find specific groups of birds, such as ducks, in other books about birds.

The quick photo guide on p. 4 will aid you in finding the main bird groups and narrowing your search.

Parts of A Bird

eyebrow

lore

chin

throat

breast

wing bars

secondary feathers

primary feathers

crown

nape

eye-line

rump

upper tail coverts

Savannah sparrow.

Species Information and Identifying Features

Color photographs, descriptions and concise information are included for each bird.

NAME The current accepted common name and scientific or Latin name.

DESCRIPTION The most distinguishing physical features, to aid in identification.

SIZE Dimensions for large individuals of the species.

NESTING Nest site and materials, along with usual number and color of eggs.

HABITAT The type of area where the species lives, sometimes with added information if there are seasonal habitats.

Natural history notes are included for each species, offering interesting information on behavior, populations or special characteristics.

Similar Species: Distinguishing features of similar birds.

Some smaller bird species are sometimes affectionately referred to as "little brown jobs" (LBJs) if they cannot be identified. Sandpipers, which can also be difficult to identify, are sometimes referred to as "peeps."

Tips and Techniques for Better Birding

Birdsong

Although birding can be conducted at any time of the day, the best time to observe many species, during the breeding season, is early morning while the males are singing. Listen for birdsong, since many species have distinctive calls and songs. It is possible to identify many species by voice before you can see them. This is especially true during the spring and summer, and, for some species, during the entire year.

Calling

One technique that often brings birds closer, so that you can get a better view, is to call them. Try making a repeated "swishing" sound. Other calls such as *pishh* and *Sip! Sip! Sip!* can also be effective, as well as noises made by squeaking the back of the hand in a sort of "kissing" sound. This technique should not be used excessively in one area, as it can stress breeding birds.

Choosing Equipment

Binoculars

Binoculars are an excellent tool for observing all birds. They do not have to be large or heavy—they should be powerful enough to magnify the subject sufficiently but should not be too difficult to hold steady. Binoculars are rated by both their magnification and light-gathering abilities. A pair of binoculars with a rating of 7 x 40 can magnify the subject 7 times or 700%. If you are looking for your first pair of binoculars, I recommend that you choose a pair with a wide range of vision. This will aid you greatly in getting the bird in view, a skill that takes practice to learn. A pair of binoculars with 10 power, for example, may have too narrow a field of vision for beginning birders.

The second number in the designation—40, in the 7 x 40 binoculars—is the diameter of the objective lens (in millimeters) where the light enters. The larger this number, the more light is available for viewing in low-light situations, including dusk and dawn. A good beginning pair of binoculars for birding is 7 x 35 or 7 x 40. Higher magnifications and light-gathering abilities are excellent for a second pair, once you have experience at finding the birds in your binoculars. Low-light conditions may not apply at the time of day when you are observing birds.

Be sure to talk to others about the advantages and disadvantages of their binoculars. A good way to do this is to join an outdoor club. The more you can try out various binoculars in the field, the more informed choice you will be able to make.

Spotting Scopes

Many serious birding enthusiasts use spotting scopes, because they make it possible to see more details of a bird at greater distances. A tripod or car window can be used to steady this excellent tool. Magnification begins at approximately 20 times. Excellent zoom optics are available, with which you can zero in on your subject. Spotting scopes are more costly than many binoculars, depending upon quality, magnification capability and brand.

Virtual Birding Sites

Several web sites are available to help birders find and observe birds. The following sites were available at the time this book was written (February 2004).

American Bird Center
http://www.americanbirdcenter.com/

Backyard Birdwatching Almanac
http://www.suite101.com/linkcategory.cfm/10080/25542

Virtual Birder (Rare Bird Alerts)
http://www.virtualbirder.com/vbirder/realbirds/index.html

North American Bird Sounds
http://www.naturesongs.com/birds.html

Attracting Birds to Your Home

Food

Giving birds a nutritious meal is an excellent way to bring them close to your home and garden and to experience the wonders of nature. Many people think that if ducks or other birds eat bread or crackers, it must be OK to give it to them. But no birds should be fed bread, crackers, chips or similar foods meant for people. These items have no nutritional value, so they actually rob the birds of the nourishment they need to migrate or to survive the winter. A variety of wild bird seed is available at specialty stores.

It is very gratifying to attract birds year-round and observe them on a regular basis. Select foods that are appropriate for the species you wish to attract. Place your feeder at a site where you can observe the birds but not startle them while they feed. Elevate the feeding area so that the birds can watch for predators, including domestic cats, and place it away from cover such as trees, to prevent cats from capturing "your" birds. At times, hawks and owls may also frequent a feeder, to find an easy meal.

Birdhouses

Many species of birds, including wrens, swallows and tree-nesting ducks, will readily accept an appropriate man-made birdhouse as a place to raise a family. See the references listed on p. 89 for tips on building birdhouses. Feeders and birdhouses are also available commercially.

Gardening to Attract Birds

Several trees, shrubs, herbs and other native plants attract many species of birds and satisfy some of their seasonal needs. Plants can provide seeds, berries and nectar, as well as nesting sites and/or materials.

In the west, several native wildflowers, such as columbine (*Aquilegia* spp.) and penstemon (*Penstemon* spp.) are favorites of hummingbirds. Native plants that attract seed- and fruit-eating birds include birch (*Betula* spp.), dogwood (*Cornus* spp.), hawthorn (*Crataegus* spp.) and chokecherry (*Prunus virginiana*). In addition, several non-native plants that attract birds are available at nurseries.

However, please note that some plants, such as bracted honeysuckle (*Lonicera involucrata*), produce berries that are **poisonous to humans**, and are best avoided if they would be within reach of small children.

Common Loon *Gavia immer*

DESCRIPTION Summer: Head black; neck black with a striped white necklace; back black with rows of white spots.
SIZE Length to 32" (80 cm).
NESTING Nest: At water's edge, made from various aquatic plants piled in the water. **Eggs:** Normally 2, olive spotted with brown.
HABITAT Breeds on fresh-water lakes.

The distinctive mournful call of the common loon is often heard near lakes, where it breeds. The population of this species has been reduced, especially in the southern portion of its range. It migrates along the Pacific coast and inland as it makes its way to and from its breeding grounds, as far north as Alaska. Loons dive to a depth of 264' (80 m) and have been clocked at speeds of 75 mph (120 km/h) while flying on migration.

Pied-billed Grebe *Podilymbus podiceps*

DESCRIPTION Overall chicken-like body shape with short bill. **Summer:** Brown; throat patch black; eyes dark, each with a white eye-ring; bill short and white with a dark black ring.
SIZE Length to 13½" (34 cm).
NESTING Nest: Attached to live aquatic plants, near surface of water; made from decaying vegetation. **Eggs:** Normally 4–7, bluish green.
HABITAT Ponds, lakes and marshes.

The pied-billed grebe is a solitary and secretive species that is famous for its wide array of vocalizations during the breeding season in spring. Included in its repertoire is a loud and distinctive *kuk-kuk-kuk cow cow cow cowp cowp cowp*, along with various cooing noises and a gobbling call. It is a small grebe, and amazing in its ability to sink slowly into the water, submerging itself completely or up to its neck.

Horned Grebe *Podiceps auritus*

DESCRIPTION Breeding adult:
Neck chestnut; horn-like tufts golden.
SIZE Length to 15" (38 cm)
NESTING Nest: In shallow water, made from aquatic vegetation.
Eggs: Normally 4–6, white to pale green or buff.
HABITAT Shallow lakes and ponds.

This grebe is a solitary species that seldom nests in colonies. It also inhabits Eurasia, where it is called the Slavonian grebe.

   Males and females share the duties of incubating the eggs. Once hatched, all young grebes have a small triangular patch of skin on the top of their heads. This patch changes to deep red as the chick gets excited, such as when it is begging its parents for food. It is likely a stimulus for the parents to feed their young.

Similar Species: The eared grebe (*Podiceps nigricollis*) is a gregarious species that often nests in colonies. It has a black neck and a golden tuft of feathers that fan out behind and below the eye.

Red-necked Grebe *Podiceps grisegena*

DESCRIPTION Breeding adult:
Throat and cheeks white; fore-neck reddish.
SIZE Length to 20" (50 cm).
NESTING Nest: Floating nest, made from fresh and decayed vegetation and attached to live plants; solitary or in colonies.
Eggs: Normally 4–5, bluish white.
HABITAT Shallow lakes and wetlands during breeding season.

As in all grebes, the legs of the red-necked grebe are positioned far back on the body. This placement is excellent for swimming, but in order to fly, the bird requires a stretch of open water approximately 165' (50 m) long for takeoff. This limits the areas where the species can nest. The red-necked grebe nests alone or in loose colonies in shallow lakes and similar areas. Courtship practices include the male presenting aquatic vegetation to the female. When the young are still very small, they may be observed catching a ride on a parent's back. Common loons (p. 11) have been known to harass red-necked grebes at both nesting and hunting areas.

Western Grebe *Aechmophorus occidentalis*

DESCRIPTION Overall black upper parts and white lower parts; head with distinctive black cap; neck long and narrow.
SIZE Length to 25" (63 cm).
NESTING Nest: Floating nest, made from fresh and decayed vegetation and attached to live plants; in colonies. **Eggs:** Normally 2–4, pale bluish white.
HABITAT Breeds on large lakes.

The western grebe uses its long bill to spear fish, the mainstay of its diet. It is normally a gregarious bird, nesting in groups with up to 90 pairs in a colony. The courtship display is truly spectacular—the birds perform their water ballet by skittering upright along the surface of the water. The ritual is enacted by a mated pair of birds, or two males, or (occasionally) one female accompanied by two males.

American White Pelican *Pelecanus erythrorhynchos*

DESCRIPTION Adult: White with black primaries; bill yellow to bright orange.
SIZE Length to 62" (1.5 m).
NESTING Nest: On the ground, on islands. Nests in colonies. **Eggs:** Normally 2, dull white.
HABITAT Lakes, rivers and marshes.

The bill of the American white pelican can hold up to an amazing 3 gallons (12 L) of water. Like all pelicans, it is a fisher. It uses its large bill to trap fish along with water, which slowly drains out, leaving the fish behind. Several white pelicans often feed together, to improve the efficiency of this technique. Most fish they capture are minnow-sized, but this species has been known to capture fish as large as 4½ pounds (2 kg).

With a wingspan reaching an impressive 10' (3 m), this pelican is well known for its soaring and gliding abilities, traveling as far as 100 miles (160 km) in search of food for their young. A temporary horn grows on the upper bill but drops off during the incubation of eggs.

Double-crested Cormorant *Phalacrocorax auritus*

DESCRIPTION Adult: Black overall; throat yellow-orange. **Breeding adult:** Crown with two tufts.
SIZE Length to 32" (80 cm).
NESTING Nest: On the ground, often on an island or on a man-made structure. Nests in colonies. **Eggs:** Normally 3–4, bluish white.
HABITAT Lakes inhabited by fish.

In the world of the double-crested cormorant, the changing of the guard at the nest site is an elaborate and romantic endeavor. The bird that has rested flies to the nest, parades regally around the sitting partner, then tenderly nudges it and eventually places its head under the wing of the sitting bird. The sitting bird then flies off to join other cormorants.

This species is a summer resident in areas where there is a good source of fish. After fishing, they often stretch their wings out to dry in the sun, since they do not have a natural waterproofing for their feathers. Like members of the owl clan, cormorants regurgitate pellets that contain indigestible materials such as fish bones.

Both pelicans and cormorants incubate their eggs in an unusual manner compared with other species. They use their webbed feet, rather than a brood patch (a bare patch of skin on the breast), to cover the eggs and keep them warm.

American Bittern *Botaurus lentiginosus*

DESCRIPTION Adult: Upper parts rich brown; neck highlighted with a black streak.
SIZE Length to 28" (70 cm).
NESTING Nest: Above shallow water in thick marsh growth. **Eggs:** Normally 3–5, pale brown to olive-buff.
HABITAT Prairie ponds, marshes and similar areas.

The American bittern is well known for its distinctive *onk-a-BLONK* call, which may be heard .6 mile (1 km) away. It is also well known for its habit of "hiding" from intruders by pointing its bill and head skyward and remaining motionless. Its coloration also greatly aids it in staying inconspicuous among the cattails and similar marsh vegetation. The male may mate with two or three females during the breeding season. Like many species that require marshlands, this species is declining in numbers as their habitat is reduced and eliminated.

Great Blue Heron *Ardea herodias*

DESCRIPTION Back and wings blue-gray; head white with black bar above eye; legs and neck very long.
SIZE Length to 46" (115 cm).
NESTING Nest: In a tree, made from sticks; in colonies. Usually to 20–60' (6–18 m) off the ground, occasionally more than 100' (30 m) up.
Eggs: Normally 3–5, pale blue.
HABITAT Fresh-water shorelines.

The great blue heron, a striking bird, is commonly seen throughout much of North America. It is an expert fisher that is often observed standing in shallow water, patiently waiting for the right moment to strike. This heron feeds on fish, but also on frogs, salamanders, shrews and voles. If disturbed at a fishing site, it creates a great commotion, uttering a series of prehistoric-sounding shrieks—seemingly in anger at the intruder—before flying off.

Herons' courtship rituals include elaborate displays and presentations of sticks. Their colonies are easily disturbed and should not be approached, because great blue herons abandons their nests with little provocation.

Tundra Swan *Cygnus columbianus*

DESCRIPTION Adult: White overall; neck elongated; bill and forehead form a straight ridge; bill black with a small yellow skin patch.
SIZE Length to 52" (1.3 m).
NESTING Nest: On the ground, near water. **Eggs:** Normally 4–5, pale green.
HABITAT Lakes and other wetlands.

The tundra swan, as its name suggests, migrates through the area while on its way to breeding grounds in the Arctic, where the male does 75% of the incubating. This magnificent species was hunted for its feathers in the 19th century, but its numbers have since recovered. The best way to identify this species is by its voice, which resembles the sound produced by reed instruments.

Similar Species: The trumpeter swan (*Cygnus buccinator*), a very similar swan, may be observed in the same area. This species has a distinctive voice that can be described as deep and resonant, similar to the sound of a French horn.

Snow Goose *Chen caerulescens*

DESCRIPTION White overall; neck slender, wings with black tips.
SIZE Length to 28" (70 cm).
NESTING Nest: On a ridge or hummock; in colonies. **Eggs:** Normally 3–5, whitish.
HABITAT Various areas on migration.

Fall brings skeins or flocks of snow geese to the west. These annual migrations are an impressive sight, accompanied by an equally impressive noisy, excited clamor. Snows are known to cruise to altitudes as great as 6,000' (1,800 m) while on migration. There are two color phases of this species: white and blue (rarely observed in the west). The total population has increased dramatically in recent years.

Canada Goose *Branta canadensis*

DESCRIPTION Back and wings brown; head and neck black with a distinctive white chin-strap.
SIZE Length to 45" (114 cm).
NESTING Nest: On the ground near water, in a tree, up to 102' (31 m) off the ground, or at the edge of a cliff. Nest is made of sticks, grass and moss, and lined with down. **Eggs:** Normally 4–7, white.
HABITAT Fresh-water areas.

The Canada goose is a common year-round resident over much of North America. Its numbers have increased steadily, largely because of the work of biologists and the availability of large new feeding areas such as golf courses. Today their nests can also be found within the boundaries of many cities. Canada geese mate for life and are known to live as long as 30 years. They usually feed on a variety of vegetation, and young geese gain weight rapidly and fledge in 63 days. Their migration is characterized by flying "V" formations.

Green-winged Teal *Anas crecca*

DESCRIPTION Adult: Speculum green. **Breeding male:** Gray overall; head cinnamon with an iridescent green ear patch. **Female:** Brown overall.
SIZE Length to 14½" (36 cm).
NESTING Nest: On the ground, made of grasses, weeds and twigs, and lined with down. **Eggs:** Normally 6–11, cream to buff.
HABITAT Fresh-water areas.

This common species, well known for its swift flight, is a small duck, often found in small flocks. It is known to live as long as 16 years, although the average lifespan is probably shorter. Nests are located in woodland areas near wetlands. The male's voice is a distinctive high-pitched whistle, while the female's is reminiscent of the mallard's quack.

Mallard *Anas platyrhynchos*

DESCRIPTION Adult: Speculum or wing patch bright blue with white edges; legs and feet bright orange. **Breeding male:** Head iridescent green.
SIZE Length to 23" (58 cm).
NESTING Nest: Normally on the ground, made of reeds or grasses, and lined with down. **Eggs:** Normally 7–10, occasionally to 15, olive.
HABITAT Marshes, ponds, bogs, lakes and similar situations.

The mallard is likely the most common species of waterfowl in North America and perhaps in the entire north temperate zone. Its presence is often announced by the loud *quack, quack, quack* of the female. These ducks dine on a wide variety of foods, including aquatic vegetation, seeds and aquatic insects, and they are well known, especially by hunters, for their love of grain and corn. The mallard is a familiar sight in urban parks throughout much of North America. It is important not to feed bread to this species or any wild bird, because it has no nutritional value for birds (see p. 9).

Northern Pintail *Anas acuta*

DESCRIPTION Breeding male: Head chocolate brown; body gray; breast white; tail elongated. **Female:** Overall brown; tail pointed. **SIZE** Length to 26" (65 cm). **NESTING Nest:** On the ground, made of grasses and leaves, and lined with down. **Eggs:** Normally 6–10, pale olive. **HABITAT** Wetlands.

The pintail has been identified as the most widely distributed duck in North America. Its trademarks in the field are its long, slender neck and its long, pointed tail.

In the northern pintail, as in many birds, females are often subtle in coloration while their mates are brightly colored. This difference is believed to aid in the survival of a species. Females normally incubate the eggs, and their subdued coloration helps prevent them from being detected by predators. The bright colors of males, on the other hand, draw attention away from the female and the nest site.

Blue-winged Teal *Anas discors*

DESCRIPTION Breeding male: Head bluish gray with white crescent; wing with large blue patch and green speculum. **Female:** Brown overall; wing with large blue patch and green speculum. **SIZE** Length to 16" (40 cm). **NESTING Nest:** On the ground in open areas, made of grasses and weeds lining a depression. **Eggs:** Normally 9–13, white to olive. **HABITAT** Ponds and marshes.

The blue-winged teal is a rapid flyer with expert aviation skills, twisting and turning with fine precision in small groups. This species rarely tips up. It feeds primarily on the water surface and occasionally on the shoreline, eating mainly seeds as well as vegetative portions of aquatic plants. The blue-winged teal migrates north in late spring, and shortens its northern stay even further by returning early in the fall. Ring-necked pheasants (p. 31) have been known occasionally to lay their eggs in the nests of the blue-winged teal.

Northern Shoveler *Anas clypeata*

DESCRIPTION Breeding male: White overall; head iridescent green; body with orange patches on sides; bill large and spoon-shaped. **Female:** Brown overall; bill large and spoon-shaped.
SIZE Length to 19" (48 cm).
NESTING Nest: On the ground, near water, made of dried grasses and weeds, and lined with down. **Eggs:** Normally 9–12, pale olive.
HABITAT Marshes, ponds, bogs, lakes and similar situations.

This common puddle duck is often seen in small groups, during migration to and from the nesting areas. Courtship rituals begin with the male uttering a guttural *konk, konk, konk* while repeatedly craning his neck and raising his head. If the female approves, the two birds swim in circles, one behind the other, with water running through their bills. Eventually the female lays her eggs in a ground nest. During migration, these ducks may be observed in larger numbers feeding together in various wetlands.

Gadwall *Anas strepera*

DESCRIPTION Breeding male: Gray overall; belly white; rump black; wing patch white. **Female:** Overall a mixture of browns; belly white; wing patch white.
SIZE Length to 20" (50 cm).
NESTING Nest: On the ground, often near water, made of dried grasses and weeds, and lined with down. **Eggs:** Normally 8–10, white. Some nests contain the eggs of 2 or more females.
HABITAT Wetlands.

The gadwall often goes unnoticed because of its dull coloration, but the colors are distinctive upon close examination. The female gadwall is especially impressed with the male's speculum and black color. Gadwalls are dabblers that favor small wetlands as their resorts and breeding areas. Most are summer residents, but many individuals migrate through the area on their way to northern breeding areas. Some long-distance migrants have been known to travel as far as 1,500 miles (2,500 km) to reach their southern destination.

American Wigeon *Anas americana*

DESCRIPTION Breeding male: Gray head with a white cap and green ear patch. **Female:** Brown overall; head gray; belly white. **Adult:** White wing patch. **SIZE** Length to 19" (48 cm).
NESTING Nest: On the ground, made of dried grasses and weeds, and lined with down. **Eggs:** Normally 8–11, whitish.
HABITAT Areas near fresh water.

The American wigeon, a common summer resident of the west, feeds primarily on vegetation, especially pond weeds, grasses, algae and sedges. Large flocks are often found wintering in areas that have big grassy areas, such as golf courses. American wigeons are also known to help themselves to the food items accidentally dropped by diving water birds, including the canvasback (see below) and American coot (p. 36). The American wigeon was once called the baldpate because of the white or "bald" spot on the head.

Canvasback *Aythya valisineria*

DESCRIPTION Male: Body white; head red; forehead slopes smoothly into the long bill. **Female:** Body gray; head brownish.
SIZE Length to 21" (53 cm).
NESTING Nest: Large and basket-like, in marsh vegetation above water or on dry ground. Nest materials include a wide variety of dead plants. **Eggs:** Normally 7–12, olive.
HABITAT Fresh-water areas with abundant vegetation along the edge.

Canvasbacks feed by diving for the succulent roots of various plants found at their "lake resort." They also feed on fishes, tadpoles, leeches and snails. Much of their food is obtained from their deep dives. This species is one of our fastest ducks, moving at speeds of 72 mph (115 km/h), but it is not a vocal one. It makes a few short calls, including a growl that the male may utter during courtship. Canvasbacks have been known to live as long as 19 years.

Redhead *Aythya americana*

DESCRIPTION Breeding male: Head rounded and red; bill tri-colored; back and sides gray. **Female & eclipse male:** Dark brown overall; chin lighter in color.
SIZE Length to 19" (48 cm).
NESTING Nest: Above shallow water in dense marsh, especially with thick bulrushes. **Eggs:** Normally 9–14, white to olive buff.
HABITAT Lakes and marshes.

Redheads are known to incubate their own eggs as well as to lay eggs in the nests of other species, including canvasback, cinnamon teal, mallard and occasionally the sora (p. 36) and American bittern (p. 14). This species is so bold that a female sometimes even lays her eggs in the nest of another species when an incubating bird is sitting there. It is a case of not putting all of your eggs in one basket—letting another female incubate one or more eggs, so that a predator cannot destroy an entire clutch at once.

The redhead is also known to contribute to dump nests—nests in which several females lay their eggs. One dump nest was found to have 13 different females laying eggs in one nest; another was found to contain an unbelievable 87 redhead eggs; yet another had 74 redhead eggs along with one black tern egg—likely laid by the bird that made the nest.

Ring-necked Duck *Aythya collaris*

DESCRIPTION Male: Back dark; chest black; head purple, often appearing black. **Female:** Dark brown, white eye ring.
SIZE Length to 18" (45 cm).
NESTING Nest: On the ground or on floating vegetation. Nest materials include grass, sedges and weeds; nest is lined with down. **Eggs:** Normally 8–10, olive to buff.
HABITAT Fresh-water marshes.

The ring-necked duck is a summer resident that looks very similar to the lesser scaup (p. 22), which it often accompanies. This omnivore feeds on grain, pond weeds, water lily bulbs, frogs, insects and snails. Individuals gather into flocks by early May to migrate to their breeding grounds inland. The ring on this species is so difficult to see that perhaps it should be called ring-billed duck.

Lesser Scaup *Aythya affinis*

DESCRIPTION Breeding male: Back gray; chest black; head purple (may also show some green). Head is triangular in shape with a peaked crown. **Female:** Brown overall; head with a white patch adjacent to the bill.
SIZE Length to 16½" (41 cm).
NESTING Nest: On the ground, often on an island, made from dry grass, lined with down. **Eggs:** Normally 9–11, olive-buff.
HABITAT Primarily near smaller bodies of fresh water deep enough for diving ducks.

The lesser scaup is a summer resident that is found throughout the area. It is a common duck that nests on islands when they are available. Meal selections include such gourmet items as worms, fry, water insects and larvae. The flight of the lesser scaup is well known for its erratic pattern, with much twisting and turning.

Harlequin Duck *Histrionicus histrionicus*

DESCRIPTION Breeding male: Striking harlequin-like colors. **Female:** Brown overall; head with three white areas.
SIZE Length to 16½" (41 cm).
NESTING Nest: On the ground, often near water, made of grasses and twigs, lined with down. **Eggs:** Normally 5–7, pale buff.
HABITAT Along the coast and mountain streams.

Harlequin ducks bounce around like corks in the water. For breeding, they favor areas with the roughest of mountain streams. They sometimes get broken bones while being tossed about, but the bones usually mend. Males accompany females to the breeding grounds but do not assist in raising young; instead they return to the coast. The females return to the coast later with that year's young.

The diet of harlequins changes with the seasons. While on the breeding grounds, they feed on aquatic invertebrates such as the larvae of stoneflies, midges and others. Like American dippers (p. 66), they can walk along the bottoms of streams, feeding underwater for up to half a minute. In some areas, boating activity on sensitive breeding streams interferes with reproduction and feeding.

Common Goldeneye *Bucephala clangula*

DESCRIPTION Breeding male: Back and wings black barred with white; breast white; head dark with greenish sheen and a round white spot on the cheek; eyes golden. **Female:** Brown overall; head dark brown.
SIZE Length to 20" (50 cm).
NESTING Nest: In a tree cavity, 5–60' (1.5–18 m) off the ground. **Eggs:** Normally 7–10, olive green.
HABITAT Fresh-water areas.

The common goldeneye is well known for its swift flight and the whistling sound of the air rushing through its wings. Spring courtship rituals include an elaborate head-bobbing display by the male. Females are known for their determination to find nesting spots—some have even been known to make their way down chimneys in the search. When nature's accommodation is at a premium, they use nest boxes where available, and if all else fails, two females may deposit their eggs in the same nest.

Bufflehead *Bucephala albeola*

DESCRIPTION Breeding male: Back black; lower body white; head iridescent green with a hint of purple and a white patch on the crown. **Female:** Light brown overall; head dark brown with a white spot.
SIZE Length to 13½" (34 cm).
NESTING Nest: In a tree cavity, 2–50' (.6–15 m) off the ground. **Eggs:** Normally 8–10, cream colored.
HABITAT Fresh-water areas.

This common species, which gets its name from the puffy appearance of its head, is conspicuously small and never found in large numbers. Pairs of buffleheads remain together for a considerable time and repeatedly return to the same nesting area, near water, where they use the abandoned nests of northern flickers (p. 55). Their diet is varied and includes both fish and fish eggs. The bufflehead has been known to live as long as 13 years.

Common Merganser *Mergus merganser*

DESCRIPTION Male: Head green and lacking a crest; breast white. **Female:** Light brown overall; head rust colored with a crest; breast white; distinct border between rust-colored neck and white breast.
SIZE Length to 25" (63 cm).
NESTING Nest: Usually near water, in a large tree cavity or rock crevice, or under a tree bank. **Eggs:** Normally 8–11, buff.
HABITAT Fresh-water areas.

Like others in the merganser clan, the common merganser is primarily a fish eater. The toothed bill enables this bird to capture the slipperiest of fish. Flocks of common mergansers are known to work collectively to drive fish into a bay and feast on their prize. The young of this year-round resident eat heartily, up to an impressive 80% of their body weight per day when they are only 10 days old.

Ruddy Duck *Oxyura jamaicensis*

DESCRIPTION Breeding male: Cheek patches white; bill bright blue. Tail is often stiffly cocked up; back and wings reddish brown. **Female:** Back and wings dark brown; cheek light brown with a single dark brown line below the eye.
SIZE Length to 15" (38 cm).
NESTING Nest: Platform of woven cattails and grasses placed in dense vegetation, just a few inches over water.
Eggs: Normally 5–10, white, becoming stained over time in the nest.
HABITAT Marshes, ponds and lakes.

The courtship display of the ruddy duck consists of an elaborate series of gestures. The male displays with a pumping motion of his bright baby-blue bill, an activity that increases in speed as the display progresses. The female lays immense eggs that are larger than that of the mallard, a bird that is twice as large. The ruddy duck is also a nest parasite, laying its eggs in the nests of other ruddy ducks, and in dump nests in quantities as large as an amazing 60 eggs. This species has an unusually large number of common and regional names. In one reference alone a total of 70 names are listed.

Osprey *Pandion haliaetus*

DESCRIPTION Adult: Chocolate brown above; white below; wings long and angled backward at the bend; dark line from eye to neck; distinctive black "wrists" visible from below when the bird is in flight.
SIZE Length to 25" (63 cm).
NESTING Nest: On top of a tree or snag. Nest is a platform made from sticks. **Eggs:** Normally 3, cream colored with brown blotches.
HABITAT Near lakes with fish.

The osprey is a world citizen, truly cosmo-politan in both temperate and tropical areas of the globe. With its dramatic wingspan to 6' (1.8 m), the bird hovers

above the water while hunting for fish. It is well known for its spectacular dives, often emerging from the water with an impressive fish that even a human would be proud of catching, although some fish are lost to raiding bald eagles (see below).

The osprey is well equipped to survive with many useful adaptations. Its oily feathers effectively repel water even after repeated dives. The angular shape of the wings ensures that they are not injured when the bird dives into the water at high speed. The talons are more curved than those of other birds of prey and are enhanced by spiny spicules with which the osprey can grasp slippery fish.

Bald Eagle *Haliaeetus leucocephalus*

DESCRIPTION Adult: Dark brown overall; head white; tail white. **Juvenile:** Overall dark brown; white feathers appear on the head in the fourth year and proportion of white feathers on the head increases with age.
SIZE Length 31–37" (78–93 cm).
NESTING Nest: On a cliff or in a tree, to 180' (54 m) or more off the ground. Nest is an accumulation of sticks that is added to over the years. **Eggs:** Normally 2, white.
HABITAT Along the coast and near large lakes containing fish.

The bald eagle is a grand species that always commands attention, whether it is sitting in a tree or soaring high in the sky. The bald eagle is a skillful predator, hunting fish, waterfowl and other birds on the water and remaining ever watchful for the right moment to claim its prize. And it is adept at harassing the osprey (see above), causing it to drop its fish; occasionally the eagle will catch the fish at lightning speed before it touches the water. This large bird of prey can use thermals to circle at amazing heights.

Sharp-shinned Hawk *Accipiter striatus*

DESCRIPTION Male: Dark blue above; barred breast; wings rounded; tail long, barred and noticeably squared off. **Female:** Dark brown above.
SIZE Length 9–13" (23-33 cm).
NESTING Nest: Usually in a conifer, 20–60' (6–18 m) off the ground. Nest is made from sticks and lined with strips of bark. **Eggs:** Normally 4–5, white with brown blotches.
HABITAT Forested areas and woodlands.

Fear reigns among many forest birds when this little resident predator is nearby. The sharp-shinned hawk sits quietly on a perch in a wooded area, waiting for its prey, and then chases small birds, dodging branches as it goes. The similar-sized merlin (see p. 30) does not actively hunt by chasing its prey through trees.

Females are much larger and weigh almost twice as much as males. Their prey also differs significantly: females tend to take birds the size of grosbeaks, while males are often successful with junco-sized birds.

Cooper's Hawk *Accipiter cooperii*

DESCRIPTION Similar to sharp-shinned hawk (see above) but larger; slate-gray above; tail longer, barred and rounded; head with black cap.
SIZE Length 14–19" (35–48 cm).
NESTING Nest: In a tree, 25–50' (7–15 m) off the ground, made from sticks and lined with bark strips. **Eggs:** Normally 3–5, bluish white with dark markings.
HABITAT Forested areas and woodlands.

Closely related to the sharp-shinned hawk (see above), the Cooper's hawk is larger overall with a longer tail. This hawk feeds primarily on birds as big as ducks, and some small mammals. It is often seen sitting out in the open, waiting to attack its prey rather than chasing it.

Cooper's hawks were once among the most common hawks in North America, but its numbers are declining. Some biologists believe that the reduction in populations of small birds may be the prime cause.

Northern Goshawk *Accipiter gentilis*

DESCRIPTION Adult: Dark gray above; light gray below; cap dark; eyebrow white.
SIZE Length to 26" (65 cm).
NESTING Nest: In a tree, usually 25–50' (7–15 m) off the ground. Nest materials include sticks of various sizes and green foliage. **Eggs:** Normally 2–4, bluish fading to white.
HABITAT Coniferous and mixed-wood forests.

The northern goshawk is noted for vigorously defending its nest from a variety of enemies, including people—a confrontation that can draw blood. This powerful predator hunts inside the forest, often perching on branch until prey is spotted. At this point, the bird flies off to pursue the prey with a short burst of amazing speed, swerving to avoid branches and often crashing through thickets. At the nest, the female remains with the young while the male hunts and brings home the food.

Populations of the northern goshawk are declining, probably because of loss of habitat.

Swainson's Hawk *Buteo swainsoni*

DESCRIPTION Adult: Back and wings dark brown; underparts whitish to light brown; bib dark brown; flight feathers dark brown.
SIZE Length to 21" (53 cm).
NESTING Nest: Platform of sticks in a tree, 15–30' (4.5–9 m) off the ground. **Eggs:** Normally 2–3, bluish white with brown spots.
HABITAT Prairie, open grasslands and similar areas.

The Swainson's hawk consumes a wide range of foods, including rodents and birds. Large insects, such as grasshoppers and caterpillars, are also important prey while the hawk is wintering in South America. This species has suffered great losses in its population because of insecticides used in Argentina, its winter range.

On the prairies, where one lone tree may be the only nest site for miles around, the Swainson's hawk or ferruginous hawk (p. 28) is often found nesting. Swainson's hawks often occupy old black-billed magpie (p. 61) nests to raise their young.

Red-tailed Hawk *Buteo jamaicensis*

DESCRIPTION Adult: Dark-brown above; upper surface of tail normally brick red; dark belt across the abdomen.
SIZE Length to 24" (60 cm).
NESTING Nest: In a tree, to 120' (36 m) off the ground, made from sticks and lined with fine materials. **Eggs:** Normally 2–3, white with brown blotches.
HABITAT Forested areas.

The red-tailed hawk is a common and widespread bird of prey found throughout much of North America. Often observed sitting on a treetop or a telephone pole, this hawk is ever watchful for its next meal. Courtship rituals often include elaborate dives and other aerial acrobatics. The bird emits a distinctive harsh scream, sometimes transcribed as *keeeeer*, while it circles above the ground. Its diet includes mice, voles, ground squirrels, rabbits, small birds, garter snakes and occasionally insects. Like so many other raptors, this species was persecuted for years and now is protected, performing a valuable service by controlling rodents in agricultural areas. The red-tailed hawk is known to live as long as 16 years.

Ferruginous Hawk *Buteo regalis*

DESCRIPTION Adult: Back and shoulders reddish brown; underparts whitish; leggings rusty.
SIZE Length to 23" (58 cm).
NESTING Nest: Platform of sticks in a tree, 20–50' (6–15 m) off the ground. **Eggs:** Normally 2–4, white with brown markings.
HABITAT Prairie, open grasslands and similar areas.

This prairie species is a truly the regal bird of prey that its scientific name suggests. Researchers have determined that ground squirrels make up 90% of the food in the ferruginous hawk's diet. This works out to an amazing average of 480 ground squirrels per hawk per year. Voles, mice and jackrabbits make up the remainder of its meals.

This species employs cunning hunting techniques, including crouching at the burrow entrance of a ground squirrel to grab one when it appears. The ferruginous hawk winters as far south as California and lives as long as 20 years in the wild.

Northern Harrier *Circus cyaneus*

DESCRIPTION Male: Gray-blue above; tail long; rump white; breast white and spotted. **Female:** Similar to male but with brown coloration. **Juvenile:** Similar to female but cinnamon below.
SIZE Length to 23" (58 cm).
NESTING Nest: Over shallow water or on the ground, in a field or marsh. Nest materials include sticks, grass and weeds. **Eggs:** Normally 4–6, bluish white, sometimes spotted with brown.
HABITAT Near wetlands.

Once called the marsh hawk, the northern harrier is a common inhabitant of the marsh. It carries out a seemingly endless search for food, travelling more than 60 miles (100 km) per day in search of food. Occasionally this raptor can be seen stalling in mid-flight when a slight movement is detected, then dropping into the grass to collect a treat such as a vole, young bird, frog or grasshopper. The northern harrier flies slowly and near the ground, except during the breeding display and while on migration. Males are well known for their swooping "skydancing" moves early in the breeding season, maneuvers that consist of vertical climbs and dives directed to prospective mates. Males are often polygamous, mating with as many as three females.

The northern harrier normally nests in wetlands, many of which are now being lost to development.

American Kestrel *Falco sparverius*

DESCRIPTION Adult: Back reddish brown; wings bluish; face white with two black stripes; breast buff-colored with black spots.
SIZE Length to 10½" (26 cm).
NESTING Nest: In a tree cavity, 10–30' (3–9 m) off the ground. **Eggs:** Normally 4–6, pale brown with brown and gray spots.
HABITAT Woodland edges, open sites and similar areas.

The American kestrel is North America's smallest falcon. It is well known for its ability to hover while it hunts for its next meal. It feeds on a wide variety of freshly killed foods, including grasshoppers, beetles, shrews, mice and frogs, but rarely birds. This vocal falcon can be recognized by its commonly heard high-pitched call, *killy-killy-killy*. It is a summer resident that migrates to the warmer climates of Central and South America for winter. Specially constructed nest boxes have been found acceptable by this species for nesting and raising a family.

Merlin *Falco columbarius*

DESCRIPTION Male: Light blue above; wings long and pointed; tail long with four black bars; breast streaked with brown. **Female:** Similar but brown overall; larger than male.
SIZE Length to 12" (30 cm).
NESTING Nest: In the abandoned nest of a hawk or crow, 10–60' (3–18 m) off the ground. No new nest materials are usually added. **Eggs:** Normally 4–5, whitish with reddish brown markings.
HABITAT Forested areas.

The merlin often occupies the abandoned nest of another species such as the American crow (p. 62), but it is very adaptable and may also take up residence on a cliff ledge or in a tree cavity. It is a falcon that normally hunts alone, but has been reported to hunt cooperatively with other merlins. In urban areas it frequently feeds on house sparrows (p. 87). It is reputed to be a belligerent raptor that will not tolerate other birds of prey in its vicinity.

The female merlin is larger than the male. Size is an important consideration to identify this species. Formerly called the pigeon hawk, this small falcon is quite vocal, often heard before it is seen with a high-pitched *ki ki ki ki ki ki ki ki*.

Peregrine Falcon *Falco peregrinus*

DESCRIPTION Black to bluish above; barred below; wings slender; tail long; head with distinctive dark sideburns.
SIZE Length to 18" (45 cm).
NESTING Nest: On a cliff ledge or tall building. No nest is made. **Eggs:** Normally 3–4, reddish brown with dark brown blotches.
HABITAT Along rivers.

The peregrine falcon is often observed quietly sitting on a snag watching for an unwary duck or shorebird. It is the fastest bird in the world, capable of reaching estimated speeds of 200 mph (320 km/h) during a stoop (closed-wing dive). With this speed, the peregrine can kill its prey instantly in the sky, and it has also been reported to catch it in mid-air. The peregrine rarely hunts birds that are sitting on the water; it waits until they take flight, when they are much more vulnerable.

This raptor nests early in the season. It selects a cliff ledge or similar spot, protected from the elements, to raise its young. In many cities today, with the help of humans, peregrines nest on high-rise buildings. Thanks to these protected nesting sites and a diet of rock doves (see p. 45), peregrine falcon populations have increased. The peregrine is known to live as long as 14 years.

Ring-necked Pheasant *Phasianus colchicus*

DESCRIPTION Breeding male: Iridescent bronze body; head dark green with red comb and skin surrounding eye; tail very long and pointed.
SIZE Length to 33" (83 cm).
NESTING Nest: On the ground. Nest is a depression lined with grass and similar materials.
Eggs: Normally 10–12, buff.
HABITAT Thickets next to agricultural crops.

In the springtime, the magnificent male ring-necked pheasant crows and beats his wings in order to advertise his presence to other males and his harem of females. During courtship, his comb becomes erect and the bare skin around his eye becomes vivid red. This year-round resident, an introduced species from China, has been brought to North America many times, for purposes of sport hunting. Numbers of the ring-necked pheasant are currently dwindling due to loss of habitat and predation by coyotes.

Spruce Grouse *Falcipennis canadensis*

DESCRIPTION Adult male: Back and wings mottled brown; throat and breast dark; eye combs red. **Female:** Underparts have black bars and white spots.
SIZE Length to 16" (40 cm).
NESTING Nest: On the ground, under dense cover. **Eggs:** Normally 5–7, olive to buff-white with brown blotches.
HABITAT Open coniferous forests and muskegs.

The spruce grouse is not often considered a culinary delight. Its primary food in winter is conifer needles, and its flesh has been said to taste like turpentine. As a result, this bird doesn't need to fear large predatory mammals. In fact, is often called fool hen since it has no fear of humans.

In a striking courtship display, the male shows off his crimson combs, along with an erect and spread tail, to the female. Once nesting has begun, the male plays no part in the incubation of the eggs or rearing of the young.

The Franklin's grouse, a western race of this species, lives in the mountains. It performs an aerial display at the end of which it slaps its wings together over its back, making a sound that resembles two loud claps. This cracking sound has been compared to the sound of a large mammal breaking branches as it moves through the forest.

Blue Grouse *Dendragapus obscurus*

DESCRIPTION Breeding male:
Sooty gray; orange comb above
eye; neck patch purple or yellow
with a white edge. **Female:**
Mottled brown.
SIZE Length to 20" (50 cm).
NESTING Nest: On the ground,
under shelter such as a log or
ledge. Nest materials include
twigs, conifer needles and leaves.
Eggs: Normally 5–10, buff with
brown speckles.
HABITAT Mountain forested areas.

The blue grouse is a year-round
resident of considerable size. The
male produces a deep, resonant
hoot, hoot, hoot as part of the
breeding display. When his neck patch is inflated, the sound is amplified and can be
heard at quite a distance. The male's display also includes raised eyebrows and a neck
patch that becomes vivid purple. This grouse has even been known to display toward a
human being when the color of the person's clothes is similar to that of the male's neck
patch. In some areas the blue grouse migrates uphill and downhill seasonally.

White-tailed Ptarmigan *Lagopus leucurus*

DESCRIPTION Summer: Brown
and white; eye comb red; tail
white. **Winter:** Overall white,
including tail.
SIZE Length to 12½" (31 cm).
NESTING Nest: On the ground,
made from various plants and
other materials, lined with
feathers. **Eggs:** Normally 2–8,
cinnamon with brown speckles.
HABITAT Mountainous regions.

The white-tailed ptarmigan, a
member of the grouse clan, is a
year-round resident of the mountains. It summers in alpine regions,
and migrates over short distances
and elevations to its winter range. Its coloration is a remarkably effective camouflage.
This species can be found farther south than any other ptarmigan in North America. Buds
form an important part of its winter diet.

Because ptarmigans live in cold, harsh environments, their toes are feathered to the
tips to keep them warm in even the coldest weather.

Ruffed Grouse *Bonasa umbellus*

DESCRIPTION Adult: Brown speckled with white and black; small crest. **Breeding male:** Neck with black ruff.
SIZE Length to 17" (43 cm).
NESTING Nest: On the ground, usually next to a log or at the base of a tree, made from leaves and grass, lined with feathers. **Eggs:** Normally 9–12, buff, occasionally with brown speckles.
HABITAT Woodlands and forest regions.

The ruffed grouse is well known for its loud drumming in the springtime. As part of his breeding display, the male stands on a log with his ruffs extended, tail fanned and wings trailing. At irregular intervals, the bird beats his wings rapidly through the air to make a drumming sound. This display is a way of announcing his presence to other ruffed grouse in the area and claiming his territory.

This year-round resident feeds on the buds, seeds and fruit of a wide range of plants. It is known all over the world for its 10-year cycle: over a 10-year period its population increases rapidly for several years, then plummets, and the cycle repeats. Increases in population are followed by increases in predator numbers, which then reduce the ruffed grouse population to very low numbers. These predators include the red-tailed hawk (see p. 28) and red fox.

33

Greater Sage-grouse *Centrocercus urophasianus*

DESCRIPTION Back and wings dark brown; belly black; tail feathers long and pointed. **Male:** Large white ruff on breast; eye combs yellow.
SIZE Length to 28" (70 cm).
NESTING Nest: On the ground, under sagebrush or a large clump of grass. **Eggs:** Normally 7–9, buff with brown spots.
HABITAT Prairie with sagebrush.

The greater sage-grouse, like several species of grouse, displays in leks—sites where a group of birds gather during the breeding season to determine social hierarchy. The word lek comes from a Swedish word meaning "play." Watching these large prairie dwellers displaying at first light is an experience never to be forgotten. In the ritual of spring, the dominant males move toward the center while the younger, less experienced males remain on the periphery. The males inflate their paired air sacs, with which they make a unique sound while conducting their strutting displays. Each air sac can hold an amazing 1.1 gal (4 L) of air. At the lek, the dominant males attract females, but only 10% of the males are able to mate with females. This bird, the largest grouse in North America, feeds on sage leaves, flowers and buds—its most important year-round food.

Wild Turkey *Meleagris gallopavo*

DESCRIPTION Male: Body dark and iridescent; wattles red; breast tuft dark.
Female & juvenile: Smaller and duller in coloration; with or without breast tuft.
SIZE Length to 46" (115 cm).
NESTING Nest: On the ground, often near the base of a tree or under a shrub.
Eggs: Normally 10–15, buff with reddish brown speckles.
HABITAT Forests with adjacent open areas.

The wild turkey, the largest game bird in North America, can run an impressive 18 mph (30 km/h). It is an introduced species that has been brought into several areas and successfully established in year-round resident populations. This species is especially impressive during courtship, when the male throws his head back, pushes his breast forward, drags his wings and fans out his tail feathers. With this display the male hopes to impress one or more females in the area. Each male may have a harem of up to 10 females.

Sharp-tailed Grouse *Tympanuchus phasianellus*

DESCRIPTION Back and wings brown; underparts with scale-like pattern; eye combs yellow.
Breeding male: Neck sacs purplish when inflated.
SIZE Length to 17" (43 cm).
NESTING Nest: On the ground, under a shrub or large clump of grass. **Eggs:** Normally 5–17, buff to light brown with brown speckles.
HABITAT Prairie, grasslands, forest edges and burned coniferous forests.

The sharp-tailed grouse is a year-round resident in a wide range of habitats. The territorial display of the male, one of the elaborate spectacles of the bird world, takes place on a lek, or dancing ground, only in the springtime. The display begins when the males hold their tails up and their heads down and inflate their vocal sacs, revealing a vivid pink or purple color. The display then continues with each male furiously stomping in a ritualized pirouette on his own stage-like area. Each of these stomping dances ends with a sudden freeze in motion. As the display becomes increasingly intense, the bird's yellow comb enlarges and the pink to violet area of the neck expands.

Sora *Porzana carolina*

DESCRIPTION Adult: Back and wings brown; face, center of throat and breast black; bill yellow or greenish. **Juvenile:** Darker overall.

SIZE Length to 8¾" (22 cm).

NESTING Nest: Cup-shaped, inches from the water in thick marsh vegetation. **Eggs:** Normally 10–12, buff with brown spots.

HABITAT Cattail marshes and similar areas.

The secretive sora is likely to be heard before it is observed. Its distinctive call—*puweee, puweee*—is often repeated during breeding season. Any sudden sound, such as a splash or a rock hitting the ground, can trigger the unique "song" of the sora, which is a descending whinny. If the bird is seen, it may be only for a few moments as it flutters a short distance in the marsh, but it is a proficient flyer, migrating as far south as South America.

American Coot *Fulica americana*

DESCRIPTION Adult: Black overall; bill whitish; legs and feet from yellow to orange. **Juvenile:** Legs and feet greenish.

SIZE Length to 15½" (39 cm).

NESTING Nest: Floating nest, made of dead vegetation. **Eggs:** Normally 6–11, buff with brownish spots.

HABITAT Freshwater marshes, ponds and sloughs.

The American coot is a member of the rail family but resembles a duck. It is a summer resident that migrates north in spring from southern climates, including California and Mexico. This bird often forms large flocks during migration.

In the springtime, downy young coots are sometimes observed, but they look so different that the observer cannot always determine what species they are. Their colorful bristle-like orange down does not resemble the plumage of an adult. Eventually these downy young molt, and begin to resemble adults.

A whitish shield extends from the bill to the forehead. This shield varies greatly in shape from one individual to another and grows larger during the breeding season. The size and shape of the shield seem to play an important part in birds recognizing each other.

Sandhill Crane *Grus canadensis*

DESCRIPTION Gray overall; cap red; legs and neck very long.
SIZE Length to 41" (103 cm).
NESTING Nest: On a mound rising above water or on dry ground, made from plant material. **Eggs:** Normally 2, olive mottled with gray or brown.
HABITAT Marshes, bogs, swamps and meadows.

The sandhill crane is both a migrant and a summer resident. The migratory flights of this bird are memorable: they circle as they gain great heights, often in good voice. The distinctive musical trumpeting calls are easy to identify and can be heard more than a mile away. This crane is well known for its courtship ballet, a series of graceful jumps, which it frequently conducts while on migration. Young sandhill cranes remain with their parents for up to 10 months.

Birding Tip: To differentiate cranes from herons in flight, remember that cranes fly with their necks stretched out while herons hold their necks in an S shape.

Killdeer *Charadrius vociferus*

Adult warms its young.

DESCRIPTION Back dark brown; breast white with a double black necklace; rump reddish orange.
SIZE Length to 10½" (26 cm).
NESTING Nest: On the ground, in an open area. Nest is a depression, sometimes lined with pebbles, grass or twigs. **Eggs:** Typically 4, buff with black or brown blotches.
HABITAT A wide variety of wetlands, open fields and pastures.

The killdeer, a plover, is one of the earliest spring migrants. It places its eggs in a depression on bare ground, and both parents incubate the eggs and care for their young. The killdeer is renowned for its "broken wing" behavior to distract possible predators from the nest. When other dangers are present, such as grazing mammals that might step on the nest, the killdeer's defense is much different: it stands over the nest and scolds the intruder in order to drive it away.

American Avocet *Recurvirostra americana*

DESCRIPTION Breeding adult: Wings and back black and white; head and neck rusty.
SIZE Length to 18" (45 cm).
NESTING Nest: On bare open ground, near water. **Eggs:** 3–5 normally 4, olive-buff with brown and black blotches.
HABITAT Prairie ponds, beaches, shallow lakes, open grasslands and similar areas.

The American avocet feeds elegantly on tiny aquatic organisms. It stirs up mud and sand with its long, curved bill and filters out the food

by sweeping the tip of its bill from side to side, just under the surface of the water, with a slightly open gape. In some areas, seeds and vegetable matter are also significant food items. The female's bill is noticeably shorter than the male's, with a greater curve. This species is often found around alkaline (high salt content) lakes.

Willet *Catoptrophorus semipalmatus*

DESCRIPTION Adult: Back and wings mottled; underparts grayish-brown; belly whitish; bill black and thick; legs gray.
SIZE Length to 15" (38 cm).
NESTING Nest: On the ground, in short, dense grass. **Eggs:** Normally 4, olive to buff with brown markings.
HABITAT Wetlands next to grasslands or similar areas.

While on the wing, the willet displays a striking black and white pattern from below. Its distinctive call, *will-will willet, will-willet*, is loud and continuous. This is in sharp contrast to the quiet, calm manner of birds siting tight on nests only a few feet from a visitor. Birds on the nest are also very well camouflaged and usually remain undetected. Male and female take turns incubating the eggs, and the "changing of the guard" is preceded by the male bowing to the female.

Spotted Sandpiper *Actitis macularia*

DESCRIPTION Head and back brown; breast spotted.
SIZE Length to 7½" (19 cm).
NESTING Nest: On the ground. Nest is a depression lined with grass and moss.
Eggs: Normally 4, buff with brown blotches.
HABITAT Near fresh water.

The spotted sandpiper is a common summer resident along the shores of lakes, rivers, streams and various types of marshes. Although this species may be observed in small flocks during migration, individuals are often found alone, walking with a distinctive "teetering" motion.

Researchers have found that in some areas, where there is an abundance of males, the female spotted sandpiper lays a clutch of eggs and then leaves it with the male to incubate and raise the young. She then takes up residence with another male and lays a second clutch of eggs for that male to raise. She may repeat the pattern with as many as 5 males before settling down to remain with her "chosen one."

Sanderling *Calidris alba*

DESCRIPTION Summer: Upper parts reddish brown; underparts white.
Winter: Pale overall; back gray; belly white.
SIZE Length to 8" (20 cm).
NESTING Nest: On the ground, in an open area. Nest is a slight depression, often lined with leaves. **Eggs:** Normally 4, olive to brown with a few brown and black spots.
HABITAT Primarily sandy beaches.

This common migrant nests in the Arctic regions of North America, Europe and Asia. It is a delightful species, probably our palest shorebird, and it can be found on every continent at some time or other during the year. As with many shorebirds, each flock performs an aerial ballet that is not soon forgotten. Sanderlings probe the shorelines of larger lakes, searching for invertebrates to "fuel-up" on for their long journeys to and from their breeding grounds. They are often spotted in small flocks near lakes, while much larger flocks, numbering as high as 80,000 individuals, have been observed along the North American coast during migration.

Semipalmated Sandpiper *Calidris pusilla*

DESCRIPTION Adult: Back and wings mottled brown; throat and sides of neck white; legs black; bill stout. **Breeding plumage:** Crown, ear patch and scapulars show a touch of rufous.
SIZE Length to 6¼" (16 cm).
NESTING Nest: On the ground, on top of a mound or on an island. **Eggs:** Normally 4, whitish to olive-buff with brown and gray blotches.
HABITAT Beaches, mud flats and similar areas.

The semipalmated sandpiper is a common spring migrant travelling north in May to its nesting grounds in the Arctic tundra and returning south in July. The bird pokes and probes for invertebrates, searching for food to replenish its body fat reserves during its long migration to the Arctic tundra from as far away as Brazil and Chile. The common name semipalmated refers to the partial webbing of the bird's toes.

Least Sandpiper *Calidris minutilla*

DESCRIPTION Back dark brown; bill short; legs short and yellowish.
SIZE Length to 6" (15 cm).
NESTING Nest: On the ground, near water. Nest is a depression lined with grass. **Eggs:** Normally 4, buff with brown blotches.
HABITAT Fresh-water beaches.

The least sandpiper is the smallest sandpiper in the world. It is a common species that is found in wetlands throughout the region during migration. The birds typically roost individually or in small groups, and nest from western Alaska to Labrador. At mudflats and sand beaches, they feed on worms, small crustaceans and a variety of insects. The least sandpiper is sometimes called a "peep," a term used for any small sandpiper, especially when its identity is in question.

Pectoral Sandpiper *Calidris melanotos*

DESCRIPTION Back and wings brown; breast with prominent streaking; belly white with a "neat dividing line."
SIZE Length to 8¾" (22 cm).
NESTING Nest: On the ground, in the Arctic. **Eggs:** Normally 4, whitish to olive.
HABITAT Wetlands and similar areas.

The pectoral sandpiper's name originates from an inflatable air sac on the male's chest. This sac is puffed out while he performs a unique flight display during courtship. However, the male does not participate in nesting activities. The female is solely responsible for incubating the eggs and raising the young. This species is commonly observed while on migration to its nesting areas in the Arctic tundra from its wintering areas as far away as southern South America. It often forages in areas of heavier vegetation, where it is difficult to observe.

Common Snipe *Gallinago gallinago*

DESCRIPTION Brown overall; back striped; bill very long and straight.
SIZE Length to 10½" (26 cm).
NESTING Nest: On the ground. Nesting materials include leaves, grass and moss. **Eggs:** Normally 4, buff with dark brown blotches.
HABITAT Marshlands and grassy meadows.

Common snipe are summer residents and world citizens. Both males and females are well known for "whinnying" during their roller-coaster courtship display. This distinctive sound is created when air rushes through their stiff outer tail feathers as they dive. The common snipe is a solitary species that uses its long bill to probe for earthworms, one of its main foods. It also feeds on cutworms, leeches, grasshoppers, beetles, mosquitoes and other insects. The common snipe is normally very stealthy when not displaying, so it can startle you if you happen to flush one.

Franklin's Gull *Larus pipixcan*

DESCRIPTION Breeding adult: Head with a black hood; bill and feet red. **Winter:** Head with a half hood; bill and feet black.
SIZE Length to 14½" (36 cm).
NESTING Nest: A large floating mass of aquatic vegetation that is anchored to rooted plants. **Eggs:** Normally 3, white-buff to olive-brown with brown or black blotches.
HABITAT Prairies and marshes.

Food for the Franklin's gull includes primarily midges, flying ants and other insects captured in mid-air. It also eats earthworms, grubs, mice and fish.

Researchers have determined that the salt glands for this species vary greatly in size with the seasons. During migration they remain large for the bird's flight along the coast, and they begin to shrink when it arrives at its breeding grounds in the wetlands. Its size increases once again when it leaves the breeding area to travel south along the coast.

Mew Gull *Larus canus*

DESCRIPTION Adult: Back and wings blue-gray; head white and rounded; bill narrow and yellow; eyes dark.
SIZE Length to 16" (40 cm).
NESTING Nest: On the ground near shoreline, or in a tree to 20' (6 m) off the ground. **Eggs:** Normally 3, olive with brown blotches.
HABITAT Near fresh water.

The mew gull is a dainty species that feeds on fish, worms, insects and a variety of other gourmet items. It is noticeably smaller than most gull species observed in the area, and it is light and buoyant in flight. Although this species is a common migrant, it is not commonly seen during the summer.

This gull makes two calls, one that is sometimes described as *kyah kyah*, and another, *meew meew*, which inspired its common name.

Ring-billed Gull *Larus delawarensis*

DESCRIPTION Breeding adult: White overall with gray mantle; wing tips black; eyes and legs yellow; bill yellow with a black ring near the tip. **Juvenile:** Head and breast streaked with gray.
SIZE Length to 17½" (44 cm).
NESTING Nest: On the ground, often on an island, in colonies. Nest is made from grass, weeds and moss. **Eggs:** Normally 2–4, light brown with dark brown blotches.
HABITAT Fresh-water areas, parks and fields.

The ring-billed gull is a common species that migrates to warmer climes during the winter months. Like many gulls, this one prefers to nest on islands, frequently nesting with the California gull (see below). This species was not always as common as it is today; it is a scavenger and the growing amount of human refuse has greatly aided in expanding its numbers. In fact, it is the most abundant gull found in North America.

California Gull *Larus californicus*

DESCRIPTION Breeding adult: Back and wings blue-gray; wing tips black; bill yellow with red spot on lower bill; legs greenish to yellowish. **First year juvenile:** Head and body dark brown; bill pink with black tip; legs pink.
SIZE Length to 21" (53 cm).
NESTING Nest: On the ground, often on an island, in colonies. **Eggs:** Normally 2–3, buff, olive or brown with dark brown blotches.
HABITAT Near lakes, on farmlands and in urban centers.

The California gull is an omnivore, feeding on a wide range of items including insects, fish, refuse, and the eggs and young of other birds. This species came to the rescue of Mormon settlers in Salt Lake City in 1848, when a plague of grasshoppers threatened their crops. Today it is sometimes seen following the farmer's plow, feeding on insects. The California gull winters along the California and Baja California coast.

Common Tern *Sterna hirundo*

DESCRIPTION White overall; cap black; tail long and forked; wings with a black wedge mark on upper surface; bill and legs red.
SIZE Length to 14½" (36 cm).
NESTING Nest: In a scrape on the ground, lined with plant material.
Eggs: Normally 1–3, buff or pale blue with brown speckles.
HABITAT Fresh-water lakes and other areas.

Like all terns, the common tern differs from gulls—its close relatives—in that it dives head first into the water to catch small fish. This is a small tern that feeds primarily on fish, but it also takes advantage of other food items such as shrimp and even the occasional swallowtail butterfly. Common terns are often seen while on migration to and from their breeding grounds in Alberta, east to Newfoundland. They are delicate-looking birds, very buoyant, with a butterfly-like flight pattern.

Similar Species: Forster's tern (*Sterna forsteri*) is very similar in appearance, but its gray tail is longer with white outer edges, and the wings lack the black wedge mark on the upper surface.

Black Tern *Chlidonias niger*

DESCRIPTION Adult: Overall black.
SIZE Length to 9¾" (25 cm).
NESTING Nest: On the ground, in scattered colonies, often on an island; a floating nest of plant material in a marsh. **Eggs:** Normally 2–4, pale buff to olive with brown and black blotches.
HABITAT Fresh-water marshes, lakes and similar areas.

Black terns feed primarily on insects as well as small fish. They choose new mates each year. Males attract females by advertising with food items such as large dragonflies or small fish. Females follow and beg for food and eventually a pair is formed. After the female accepts food from the male, mating frequently takes place.

This colony nester has been observed to form large social gatherings in flight on the breeding grounds. These flock flights take place early in the nesting season and may last as long as 20 minutes.

This bird's numbers are low but stable. For this species and many others, wetland habitat destruction is the main danger.

Rock Dove *Columba livia*

DESCRIPTION Highly variable; normally back and wings gray; head dark gray; neck iridescent.
SIZE Length to 12½" (31 cm).
NESTING Nest: On a man-made structure. Nest materials include twigs and grass. **Eggs:** Normally 2, white.
HABITAT Urban environments.

The rock dove, also called pigeon, was introduced by European settlers over a century ago and is now found over much of North America. Members of the pigeon and dove family are unique in that both male and female adult birds can produce a "milk" in their digestive systems and feed it to their young.

This bird played an important role in saving the peregrine falcon (see p. 30) from extinction. Because the rock dove lives in cities, it was not contaminated with DDT and similar pesticides, as was other prey of the peregrine falcon. Those peregrines that nested in high-rise buildings in large cities were able to safely feed on rock doves.

Mourning Dove *Zenaida macroura*

DESCRIPTION Body slender; overall brown; under parts pinkish; tail long and pointed.
SIZE Length to 12" (30 cm).
NESTING Nest: On the ground or in a tree, normally to 40' (12 m) off the ground. Nest is flimsy and made from sticks. **Eggs:** Normally 2, white.
HABITAT Semi-open areas.

The distinctive song of the mourning dove, a sad-sounding cooing: *oowoo-woo-woo-woo*, is likely the origin of its common name. This dove feeds on the seeds of grasses and wildflowers. Like all birds that eat seeds, this one regularly swallows grit or small gravel to aid in digestion. In the northern limit of its range the mourning dove raises a single brood per year. In the south, however (across the southern U.S.A.), an amazing 6 broods may be produced within one year.

45

Great Horned Owl *Bubo virginianus*

DESCRIPTION Back and wings dark brown; throat white; ear tufts widely spaced; eyes yellow.
SIZE Length to 22" (55 cm).
NESTING Nest: In the abandoned nest of a hawk, eagle or crow, 20–60' (6–18 m) off the ground, usually with no new nest materials added. **Eggs:** Normally 2–3, whitish.
HABITAT Forested areas.

The great horned owl gets its name from the two tufts of feathers on its head. It is a large species and one of the earliest of all nesters, with incubation beginning in late February or early March. A person who ventures too close to an active nest may be attacked by an angry adult, which may draw blood. This owl feeds on a wide variety of mammals, including porcupines and skunks. It is a fearsome, determined hunter that is undeterred by quills and foul smells. Great horned owls hunt by dusk and by night, and smaller owl species also become the hunted.

Snowy Owl *Nyctea scandiaca*

DESCRIPTION White overall; head round. **Male:** Plumage white. **Female & juvenile:** White, with some black feathers.
SIZE Length to 23" (58 cm).
NESTING Nest: On the ground in the Arctic. **Eggs:** Normally 3–11, varying with the abundance of food, whitish.
HABITAT Open areas such as meadows and agricultural areas.

The snowy owl is always a very visible and welcome sight during the winter months. Unlike most owls, the snowy is active during daylight hours. Its diet consists of small mammals such as lemmings, mice and voles, so it appears in winter, when the numbers of small mammals are reduced in the far north where it normally lives year-round. Lemming populations in the tundra rise and fall in four-year cycles—high numbers in one year are followed by years of reduced numbers until there are virtually none. Female snowy owls may lay up to 11 eggs in years of peak lemmings, but may not breed at all in low-population years.

This bird has been known to migrate as far south as central California in search of food during years of scarcity, and they are known for their great patience in watching for small mammals. Well adapted for life in the north, the snowy's toes are covered with feathers for insulation and its white color helps to camouflage it in the winter environment.

Burrowing Owl *Athene cunicularia*

DESCRIPTION Legs noticeably long; eyes yellow. **Adult:** Barred and spotted with brown overall. **Juvenile:** Underparts buff.
SIZE Length to 9½" (24 cm).
NESTING Nest: In a burrow, dug by the owl or abandoned by a ground squirrel or other burrowing mammal. **Eggs:** Normally 7–10, white.
HABITAT Prairie, open grasslands and similar areas.

The distinctive burrowing owl feeds on insects and small mammals. In agricultural areas where the insect population is sprayed with pesticides, this species is very vulnerable to poisoning—in many areas it feeds almost exclusively on insects such as grasshoppers. This owl needs natural areas for feeding, and its nesting burrows must be left in a natural state. The burrowing owl migrates as far south as Mexico and Central America.

In southern areas of North America, these owls dig their own burrows, but in the north they occupy abandoned burrows 3–10' (1–3 m) deep, often returning year after year to the same nest. The adults have a repertoire of about 17 songs or calls, including a mournful courtship call, and the young are well known for the rattlesnake-like warning buzz that visitors hear from inside the nesting burrow.

This small predator is in turn the prey of a wide variety of larger predators, including the badger, coyote, Swainson's hawk (p. 27), northern harrier (p. 29), prairie falcon, rattlesnake and bullsnake.

Young at burrow entrance.

Northern Pygmy-owl *Glaucidium gnoma*

DESCRIPTION Brown above; crown spotted; underparts streaked; eyes yellow; tail long.
SIZE Length to 6¾" (17 cm).
NESTING Nest: In a hollow tree, often in an opening made by a woodpecker, 8–25' (2.5–8 m) off the ground. **Eggs:** Normally 3–4, white.
HABITAT Mountain areas.

The northern pygmy-owl is often observed sitting on top of a tree while being mobbed by small birds, which gather and fly at the owl in order to chase it away. In fact, that is often the manner in which birders locate this owl. Eventually the mobbing stops and the owl goes back to sleep. This bird is a predator, active at dusk and dawn and feeding principally on small birds. Two eye-like spots or nape spots are found on the back of the head.

Barred Owl *Strix varia*

DESCRIPTION Brown above; facial disk prominent; eyes dark; belly with vertical streaks.
SIZE Length to 21" (53 cm).
NESTING Nest: In a natural tree hollow, the abandoned nest of a hawk or crow, or a similar location. **Eggs:** Normally 2–3, white.
HABITAT Forested areas.

This common year-round resident occurs in forested areas throughout much of eastern North America and is rapidly expanding its range. Its voice is a distinctive sequence of hoots: *who-cooks-for-you, who-cooks-for-you-all*. Juveniles, however, emit a loud and distinctive *psssssst*, which can be heard between June and August. This call aids birders greatly in locating the barred owl. Diet is primarily forest birds and mice, but this owl also eats reptiles, fish and insects. It is one of the easier forest owls to locate because it often hunts during the day.

Great Gray Owl *Strix nebulosa*

DESCRIPTION Adult: Back and wings brown; eyes yellow; head rounded with distinct circular facial disks; throat with narrow white markings.
SIZE Length to 27" (68 cm).
NESTING Nest: Normally a platform nest, abandoned by a raven, goshawk or similar species, in a tree, 10–50' (3–15 m) off the ground. **Eggs:** Normally 2–5.
HABITAT Bogs, meadows and thick coniferous forests.

The great gray owl, the largest owl on the continent, is a nomad that inhabits northern North America as well as northern Eurasia, roaming extensively in the winter months in search of food. A diurnal bird, it is capable of capturing small mammals under the snow. Researchers have concluded that this owl can locate its prey solely by sound. This species is more common in northern areas, but it frequently moves south during the winter months in search of small mammals.

During courtship, the male presents a vole or pocket gopher to a prospective mate. If she accepts the food, the pair mate and begin nesting together. Only the female incubates the eggs and young, and the male is responsible for bringing food to the female on the nest. As well, males have been observed feeding the young for three months after they have left the nest. This owl is well known for its "tameness," often allowing humans to come quite close.

Long-eared Owl *Asio otus*

DESCRIPTION Back and wings dark brown; facial disk rufous; ear tufts closely spaced.
SIZE Length to 15" (38 cm).
NESTING Nest: In the abandoned nest of a hawk, eagle or crow, 4–30' (1–9 m) off the ground, with no nest materials added. **Eggs:** Normally 4–6, white.
HABITAT Trees near open areas.

This slender owl often goes unnoticed during the day as it sits quietly in a thicket or dense stand of trees. It feeds during the night, primarily on small mammals such as voles. Like all owls, it regurgitates pellets containing the indigestible bones and fur of its prey, which makes it easy to determine the bird's diet. This owl incubates its eggs as soon as they are laid, so the young vary greatly in age. In fact, one family might consist of some down-covered young in the nest, and others that are learning to fly. The long-eared owl can be found between central Canada and northern Baja California, Mexico.

Short-eared Owl *Asio flammeus*

DESCRIPTION Back and wings brown; face round; tufts present but small and rarely seen; underside heavily streaked; belly buff.
SIZE Length to 15" (38 cm).
NESTING Nest: On dry ground, often near a marsh. Nest materials include grass and feathers. **Eggs:** Normally 3–11, white.
HABITAT Open meadows and wetlands.

The short-eared owl is well known for its irregular, moth-like flight, and for the loud clapping display it makes during courtship by striking its wings together. This owl also produces a "song," especially during the breeding season, that has been described as a raspy, barking sound. These birds are active during the day or at night. They inhabit North and South America, Eurasia and Africa.

Northern Saw-whet Owl *Aegolius acadicus*

DESCRIPTION Adult: Brown above; underparts streaked ; crown with short stripes; eyes yellow, tail short.
Juvenile: Overall reddish; large white area between the eyes.
SIZE Length to 8" (20 cm).
NESTING Nest: In a hollow tree, often in an opening made by a woodpecker, 15–60' (4.5–18 m) off the ground.
Eggs: Normally 5–6, white.
HABITAT Forested areas.

The northern saw-whet owl is a common owl that easily goes undetected. Its small size and its habit of sleeping during the day in a shrub or tree aid it greatly in being unnoticed. The observer who does happen to see one will find that this owl is one of the few birds that allows a person to get near it.

During winter, the northern saw-whet owl has been known to capture more food than it can eat at one time, then store it in a nearby tree, where it freezes. Later, the owl thaws the food using the warmth of its body.

Common Nighthawk *Chordeiles minor*

DESCRIPTION Male: Body and wings dark gray with barring; wings pointed with white patch (pronounced in flight); tail with white bar. **Female:** Throat yellow; tail lacking white bar.
SIZE Length to 9½" (24 cm).
NESTING Nest: On the ground or on a flat-topped building. No actual nest is built. **Eggs:** Normally 2, buff with brown blotches.
HABITAT A wide variety of open areas and rooftops.

The nighthawk is often heard long before it is observed. Its distinctive call has been described as a nasal *peent*. The bird's long, slender wings give it the agility necessary to capture insects in flight, and it has a relatively large mouth to help catch insects on the wing. The nighthawk is a summer resident, and in October it makes its way south to winter hideaways in Mexico and Central America. The numbers of this species are declining in parts of its range, perhaps because of pesticide use or habitat loss.

Ruby-throated Hummingbird *Archilocus colubris*

DESCRIPTION Adult: Back and wings green.
Male: Throat (gorget) brilliant red; chin black. **Female:** Throat and chin white.
SIZE Length to 3¾" (10 cm).
NESTING Nest: In a tree or large shrub, 5–50' (1.5–15 m) off the ground. **Eggs:** 2, white.
HABITAT Woodland edges and similar areas.

The ruby-throated hummingbird feeds on nectar, insects and sap released from woodpecker borings. In some areas, sap is an important food in the early spring, when there are few flowers to provide nectar.

The male is well known for his courtship display, in which he flies back and forth in a U-shaped pendulum flight. The nest of this tiny species is walnut-sized, with tiny pea-sized eggs.

If we humans were to metabolize our foods at the same rate as hummingbirds, we would be required to eat twice our body weight daily. Or, if we prefer to eat sugar, we would need almost half our body weight in sugar every day, and our body temperature would rise to 400°C (750°F). Hummingbirds also lower their body temperature at night and go into a torpor or coma-like state of rest to conserve energy.

Calliope Hummingbird *Stellula calliope*

DESCRIPTION Adult: Upper parts greenish. **Male:** Throat streaked with purple-red. **Female:** Flanks light cinnamon; throat speckled with green.
SIZE Length to 3¼" (8 cm).
NESTING Nest: In a conifer, 6–40' (2–12 m) off the ground. Nest is made of plant down, moss, lichens and/or other materials, bound together with spider webs. **Eggs:** Normally 2, white.
HABITAT Open mountain woodlands, wooded pond edges, canyons and similar situations.

The courtship antics of the male calliope hummingbird include impressive pendulum-style swoops toward the female. The male remains with the female only until nesting begins, then moves on to other areas.

This hummingbird is primarily a summer resident of the mountains, but it has also been found nesting in gardens and orchards. It defends its territory fiercely, uttering a series of squeaks.

Rufous Hummingbird *Selasphorus rufus*

DESCRIPTION Male: Back reddish brown; tail rufous; throat iridescent reddish orange. **Female:** Tail rufous.
SIZE Length to 3¾" (9 cm).
NESTING Nest: In a conifer, 3–30' (1–9 m) off the ground. Nest is made of plant down, moss, lichens and/or other materials, bound together with spider webs. **Eggs:** Normally 2, white.
HABITAT Forest edges, mountain meadows and shores of streams.

Arriving with the first blossoms of spring, the rufous hummingbird is a true bundle of energy. The male can be observed performing dive bombs in order to impress a chosen female hidden on a lower branch. This bird's tiny nest holds 2 tiny pea-sized eggs. The young grow quickly and eventually become big enough to fill the nest completely, reshaping it as they reach fledgling size.

Like all hummingbirds, this species can fly forward, fly backward and hover. As they fly from one blossom to another, these tiny jewels feed on nectar and small insects. They are strongly attracted to hummingbird feeders that simulate red flowers in the wild. The rufous is also an aggressive species that has little tolerance for other hummingbirds. This is why people often place several nectar feeders in one area to let all hummingbirds feed.

Belted Kingfisher *Ceryle alcyon*

DESCRIPTION Male: Overall blue-gray above and whitish below with a blue-gray necklace. **Female:** Lower breast displays an orange band.
SIZE Length to 14" (35 cm).
NESTING Nest: A burrow in a bank near water, excavated by the belted kingfisher. No nest materials are added. **Eggs:** Normally 6–7, white.
HABITAT Various fresh-water areas.

The kingfisher is distinctive for its loud, raucous, rattle-like call. It is an expert fisher, adept at catching a meal by diving into the water and emerging with a small fish. The bird then returns to its favorite perch to beat the fish on a branch, and often to toss it in the air and catch it head first. Like owls, kingfishers cough up pellets containing the indigestible portions of their meals. In addition to fish, they feed on a variety of insects and mice.

Yellow-bellied Sapsucker *Sphyrapicus varius*

DESCRIPTION Adult: Head black and white; forecrown red. **Male:** Chin and throat red; underparts yellowish. **Female:** Underparts pale yellow.
SIZE Length to 8½" (21 cm).
NESTING Nest: In a tree cavity, 6–60' (2–18 m) off the ground. **Eggs:** Normally 5–6, white.
HABITAT Deciduous (especially aspen) and mixed coniferous woods.

The yellow-bellied sapsucker has a distinctive cat-like call and it drums in an irregular rhythm. Like many other woodpeckers, it provides food to its young in the nest almost constantly (every 5 to 10 minutes). It is called a sapsucker because it consumes sap as well as berries and flying insects. Most woodpecker species have very long, barbed tongues to catch and feed on insects. This bird's tongue is shorter, with hairs rather than barbs, so that it can lap up sap.

Downy Woodpecker *Picoides pubescens*

DESCRIPTION Wings black with white spots; head black with white stripes; breast and belly white; bill slender and less than half the length of the head; outer tail feathers white with a few black bars. **Male:** Nape with red bar. **Female:** Nape without red bar.
SIZE Length to 6" (15 cm).
NESTING Nest: Usually in a cavity of a dead tree, 12–30' (3.5–9 m) off the ground. **Eggs:** Normally 4–5, white.
HABITAT Forested areas.

This year-round resident is North America's smallest woodpecker. Its bill is narrower and shorter than that of the similar-looking hairy woodpecker (below). Both male and female help to excavate a nesting cavity, as well as incubate the eggs and feed their young. During the fall and winter, males and females feed in separate territories, and both select dead limbs on which to drum loudly, thus advertising their presence. Diet includes a wide range of insects, especially beetles and ants, and these birds frequent suet feeders during the winter months.

Hairy Woodpecker *Picoides villosus*

DESCRIPTION Wings black with white spots; head black with white stripes; breast and belly white; bill thickened and long-almost 3/4 the length of the head; outer tail feathers white only. **Male:** Nape with red patch. **Female:** Nape without red patch.
SIZE Length to 9¼" (23 cm).
NESTING Nest: In a tree cavity, 4–60' (1–18 m) off the ground. **Eggs:** Normally 4, white.
HABITAT Woodlands.

This year-round resident is common throughout much of North America. Dinner consists mainly of the larvae of various beetles and other insects that live in the wood of trees. Surprisingly, hairy woodpeckers occasionally also feed on fruit and seeds. The birds keep their mates all year, although separate territories are maintained by the sexes. The female normally initiates courtship activities by drumming on one of several favorite drum trees, a sound that is often heard in the fall and can be very intense at times. Human beings can hear the drumming 2,400' (720 m) away. The hairy woodpecker's most common vocalization is *jeek, jeek*, often used as a greeting, or it can be described as a hard *peek* (perhaps easier to remember). Courtship flights may be observed: a pair flies duet style, with one bird taking the lead, then the other.

Three-toed Woodpecker *Picoides tridactylus*

DESCRIPTION Adult: Back is black with white bars; sides heavily barred; underparts whitish. **Male:** Crown yellow.
SIZE Length to 8¾" (22 cm).
NESTING Nest: In a tree cavity, 5–15' (1.5–4.5 m) off the ground. **Eggs:** Normally 3–6, white.
HABITAT Mature coniferous forests.

The three-toed woodpecker drums on trees to proclaim its territory in a distinctive manner. The rate of drumming accelerates and drops in volume at the end.

   This unique species is often heard before it is seen. Quietly it flakes away the loose bark on the trunks of spruce and other conifers to feed on the variety of insects, especially the larvae of bark beetles, living beneath. Once referred to as the ladder-backed three-toed woodpecker, this species creates a new nest cavity each year.

Similar Species: Black-backed woodpecker (*Picoides arcticus*) is, as its name suggests, a similar woodpecker that lacks white markings on its back.

Northern Flicker *Colaptes auratus*

DESCRIPTION Back and wings brown barred with black; belly buff, spotted with black; rump white, very noticeable when bird is in flight; bib black. **Male:** Moustache red.
SIZE Length to 12½" (31 cm).
NESTING Nest: In a cavity of a dead tree, 6–20' (1.8–6 m) off the ground. **Eggs:** Normally 5–8, white.
HABITAT Moderately open areas.

The northern flicker often forages for snacks on the ground or in ants' nests. In fact, in the bird world it is the champion for eating ants. Scientists determined in at least one study that 45% of all foods consumed by this woodpecker were ants. One individual was found to have more than 5,000 ants in its stomach. Additional food items in the diet included a wide variety of insects and a large selection of fruits. The northern flicker is important in providing nest sites for the bufflehead (see p. 23) and other hole-nesters, which occupy the accommodations once the flickers have finished with them.

55

Pileated Woodpecker *Dryocopus pileatus*

DESCRIPTION Back and wings black; head black with white stripes and red crest. **Male:** Moustache red.
SIZE Length to 16½" (41 cm).
NESTING Nest: In a cavity of a live or dead tree, 15–80' (4.5–24 m) off the ground. No nest materials are added. **Eggs:** Normally 3–5, white.
HABITAT Mature forests. This species requires large trees for nesting.

"Prehistoric" may best describe the appearance of this large, primitive-looking bird. Its loud, powerful voice makes a sound that could be described as *wucka-wucka-wucka*. The pileated woodpecker is also known for its bursts of drumming, which can be heard at long distances. When foraging, this bird leaves a distinctive calling card. It chisels out large, distinctive rectangular holes while it feeds, primarily on ants living in the trunks of trees. Pairs of pileated woodpeckers remain together year-round and often return to the same area to nest for years. The nest is normally, but not always, chosen so that it faces either east or south. This bird is often easily approached.

Least Flycatcher *Empidonax minimus*

DESCRIPTION Upper parts olive-brown; double wing bars; conspicuous white eye-ring; throat white.
SIZE Length to 5¼" (13 cm).
NESTING Nest: In a tree, usually 25–35' (8–11 m) off the ground. Nest materials include grass, lichens and strips of bark. **Eggs:** Normally 4, creamy white with reddish brown spots.
HABITAT Open woods, aspen groves and shrubby wetlands.

The call of the least flycatcher is a distinctive *che-bec, che-bec*, which is repeated many times. Like most flycatchers, this species darts out from its perch to capture various insects—including flies, hence its name. This is the smallest flycatcher of the *Empidonax* group.

Least flycatchers make devoted parents, so much so that one female was found still sitting on her nest even though the tree she nested in had toppled. An instance of polygyny has also been reported—a male least flycatcher mated with two females. Males sometimes feed females while they are incubating eggs on the nest.

Similar Species: The alder flycatcher (*Empidonax alnorum*) inhabits alder and willow shrubs. The easiest way to identify this species is by its buzzy *fee-bee-o* song. The olive-sided flycatcher (*Contopus cooperi*), well known for its song, *quick three beers*, is found in higher elevations, recently burned forests and northern forest bogs. It dines on bees and flying ants.

Eastern Kingbird *Tyrannus tyrannus*

DESCRIPTION Adult: Head, back and wings slate gray; underparts white; crown with an orange-red patch that is occasionally visible.
SIZE Length to 8½" (21 cm).
NESTING Nest: In a deciduous tree or shrub, 7–30' (2–9 m) off the ground. **Eggs:** Normally 3–4, white to pinkish white with gray and brown blotches.
HABITAT Forest edges, roadsides and similar areas.

The eastern kingbird is noted for its aggressive behavior in defending its nest against even large predators such as the American crow (see p. 62), red-tailed hawk (see p. 28) and human beings. One kingbird was even observed to attack a low-flying airplane! As with most flycatchers, this species feeds on aerial insects by hawking, but it is also known to feed by hovering on fruit such as red-osier dogwood berries, especially during fall migration. The diet is also known to include a variety of seeds. This species arrives in this area later in spring than most other flycatchers to begin nesting.

Horned Lark *Eremophila alpestris*

DESCRIPTION Adult: Face and throat white or yellow; "horns" black; broad stripe under the eye. **Male:** Brighter overall.
SIZE Length to 7¼" (18 cm).
NESTING Nest: On the ground, near a clump of grass, rock or similar object. **Eggs:** Normally 3–4, gray to greenish white with brown blotches.
HABITAT Prairie, open grasslands, fields and similar areas.

The horned lark is well known for performing an aerial display. This display begins when the male rapidly and quietly climbs to amazing heights—325–820' (100–250 m)—where he circles and sings for as long as eight minutes. He then drops to the ground at lightning speed with his wings tucked tightly against his body to resume his normal activities. This species has a call that can be described as *su-weet*.

The female constructs the nest alone. In some areas the bird paves the dirt next to the nest, using materials such as cow dung to cover the dirt that was excavated in making the nest.

Purple Martin *Progne subis*

DESCRIPTION Male: Body dark, glossy purplish blue. **Female & juvenile:** Underparts gray.
SIZE Length to 8" (20 cm).
NESTING Nest: Commonly in apartment bird houses. **Eggs:** Normally 4–5, white.
HABITAT Towns, cities, farms and similar areas.

The purple martin leads an urban lifestyle, easily taking up residence in apartment-style houses constructed by people. This bird is an asset to man because it feeds on a variety of insects including ants, flies, dragonflies and—yes—mosquitoes. To construct a nest box for this welcome species, consult the references on p. 89 and follow the instructions to ensure that the specific nesting requirements are met. Care should also be taken to keep out other species, especially the house sparrow (p. 87) and European starling (p. 70).

Tree Swallow *Tachycineta bicolor*

DESCRIPTION Adult: Upper parts dark blue to green; rump dark; underparts white.
SIZE Length to 5¾" (14.5 cm).
NESTING Nest: In a tree cavity, abandoned woodpecker nest or nest box. Nest materials include grass, moss and pine needles; nest is lined with feathers. **Eggs:** Normally 4–7, pale pink to whitish.
HABITAT Woodlands near water.

The tree swallow is a tree-hole nester that also adapts to various man-made structures. The installation of nest boxes in many areas, to increase the population of tree swallows, has been very successful. These pleasant birds feed on an amazing number of insects, including beetles, flies, grasshoppers and dragonflies. Surprisingly, they also feed on berries and seeds when insects are less abundant. The bird lives 2.7 years on average, and the longest living individual on record died at age 8.

Similar Species: The violet-green swallow (*Tachycineta thalassina*) is a similar swallow, but it has white flank patches that extend to the edge of the rump. Its voice is more chirp-like than the fluid calls of the tree swallow.

Cliff Swallow *Petrochelidon pyrrhonota*

DESCRIPTION Adult:
Rump buffy; tail square;
throat dark chestnut
and black.
SIZE Length to 5½" (14
cm).
NESTING Nest: On a
cliff, building or similar
site with an overhang.
Eggs: Normally 4–5,
white to pale pink.
HABITAT Rivers, farms,
semi-open land and
similar areas.

Nests.

The cliff swallow, also known as the legendary swallow of Capistrano, is a colonial nester and the master mud mason of the bird world. To build the distinctive gourd-like nest, swallows gather and apply mud, one billful at a time. At the initial stages of nest building, they commonly hover in order to anchor the nest securely. With their bills they roll the mud into balls, which are then pressed into place. One colony may have as many as hundreds or thousands of nests. In some areas the birds reuse the nests for years.

Similar Species: The bank swallow (*Riparia riparia*) displays a brown necklace-like band across its white chest. This species nests in holes in stream banks and similar sites.

Barn Swallow *Hirundo rustica*

DESCRIPTION Back and wings dark
blue; throat reddish brown; underparts buff; tail deeply forked.
SIZE Length to 6¾" (17 cm).
NESTING Nest: Usually in a sheltered
location, in a man-made structure.
Nest is made from mud and grass,
and lined with feathers. **Eggs:**
Normally 4–5, white with brown
speckles.
HABITAT In old buildings and similar
structures.

The barn swallow is a common summer resident throughout most of
North America, lingering on the breeding grounds longer than other swallows. One may wonder where the barn swallow nested before human beings provided buildings. Archival field notes and other nesting records show that nesting sites included rock caves, rock cliffs and other natural cavities. These sites may once again become important, as the numbers of barn swallows have declined. Long gone are the days when barns were com-monplace—farm and other rural buildings are fewer and farther between.

Gray Jay *Perisoreus canadensis*

DESCRIPTION Adult: Wings, tail and back dark gray; head white with a black patch at the back; breast white. **Juvenile:** Body dark gray.
SIZE Length to 11½" (29 cm).
NESTING Nest: In a conifer, 6–28' (2–8.5 m) off the ground. Nest is made from twigs and bark, and lined with feathers and fur. **Eggs:** Normally 3–4, greenish with brown blotches.
HABITAT Generally forests at higher elevations.

This friendly member of the jay clan is familiar to all who travel in the backcountry. It was formerly called the Canada jay, as well as the colloquial names whiskey jack, moose bird and camp robber. The gray jay is widespread and a year-round resident. It nests early in subalpine regions, and incubates its eggs while there is still heavy snow. The young are often fledged about the same time as the snow melts. The gray jay uses its saliva to wrap insects and stick them to branches during the fall and summer, to eat when other food is not abundant.

Blue Jay *Cyanocitta cristata*

DESCRIPTION Adult: Wings blue with white patches and black bars; head blue with crest.
SIZE Length to 11" (27 cm).
NESTING Nest: In a tree, 8–30' (2.5–9 m) off the ground. **Eggs:** Normally 4–5, green to buff with brown and gray spots.
HABITAT Deciduous and mixed woods.

Blue jays are common birds that are often observed at bird feeders. This jay is particularly adept at holding down a peanut with its feet and pecking at it to extract the morsel inside. It is also skilled at holding a hazelnut while it is still attached to the branch, letting its weight help in removing the nut from the branch, then holding it down to peck it open. In years when forest tent caterpillars (*Malacosoma disstria*), are abundant, blue jays feed hundreds of pupae to their young.

The blue jay is also well known for its anting behavior—placing ants or ant excretions on its feathers while preening in sensitive spots such as under its wing. The ant matter is believed to have a soothing effect on the bird's skin. Anting activity has been observed in at least 100 species of birds.

Clark's Nutcracker *Nucifraga columbiana*

DESCRIPTION Body gray; wings black with white patch; tail black with white outer feathers.
SIZE Length to 12" (30 cm).
NESTING Nest: In a coniferous tree, 8–40' (2.5–12 m) off the ground. Nest is made from twigs and bark, and lined with grass and pine needles.
Eggs: Normally 2–4, greenish speckled with brown and gray.
HABITAT Mountainous areas above 3,000' (900 m).

Clark's nutcrackers reside in the mountains near timber line. They are omnivores, consuming large numbers of seeds, especially from whitebark and limber pines, and a wide variety of insects, spiders, small mammals and probably carrion. In one year, an individual normally hides some 30,000 seeds in 7,500 different spots to eat later, and has a remarkable 70% success rate in relocating these seeds. Clark's nutcrackers are opportunists, often on the lookout for handouts from visitors. But keep in mind that they should only eat natural foods, because many processed human foods will not give them the nutrients they require.

Black-billed Magpie *Pica hudsonia*

DESCRIPTION Black and white overall; tail long with iridescent green highlights; wings also with iridescent green highlights; bill black.
SIZE Length to 19" (48 cm).
NESTING Nest: In a tree, 15–30' (4.5–9 m) off the ground. Nest materials include sticks, mud, weeds, grass and hair. **Eggs:** Normally 6–7, greenish with brown blotches.
HABITAT Aspen and shrubby areas with tall growth.

The black-billed magpie is a striking species, always bringing great excitement to those who have never seen it. This species builds a large, distinctive, elaborate domed nest and reuses it year after year, adding to it during each use. The great horned owl (p. 46) often nests on top of an abandoned black-billed magpie nest, although the dome is thought to be important in protecting the residents from raids by various species of owls. The female is solely responsible for the incubation of the eggs.

Clues to the diet of the black-billed magpie can be found in the pellets it regurgitates soon after eating. These pellets may include meadow vole bones, grain hulls, pits, seeds and human refuse.

American Crow *Corvus brachyrhynchos*

DESCRIPTION Black overall; bill slender and smaller than that of the raven; tail rounded.
SIZE Length to 17½" (44 cm).
NESTING Nest: In a tree, 10–70' (3–21 m) off the ground. Nest materials include sticks, mud, weeds, grass and feathers. **Eggs:** Normally 4–6, greenish with brown and gray blotches.
HABITAT Areas with mature trees for roosts and nesting.

The American crow is a common migrant and summer resident throughout much of the area. Crows' nests in trees are an important source of nesting sites for a variety of other species, including the great horned owl (see p. 46), merlin (p. 30) and Canada goose (p. 16). The American crow is a smart bird that has withstood persecution by human beings and continues to thrive.

Common Raven *Corvus corax*

DESCRIPTION Black overall; bill very thick; throat feathers long and pointed; tail wedge-shaped.
SIZE Length to 26½" (66 cm).
NESTING Nest: On a cliff ledge or in a tall tree. Nest is made from sticks and lined with grass, moss and hair. **Eggs:** Normally 4–6, greenish with brown blotches.
HABITAT All habitats.

The common raven is a widespread, year-round resident of the west. Its voice is a hoarse and raspy *kwawk*, compared to that of the American crow, which is more of a *caw*. The raven can also be called the ballet star of the Corvid family (the crow and jay clan). Gliding, soaring, barrel-rolling and diving are all part of ravens' routine, and they seem to enjoy flying. Their courtship rituals, which take place as early as February, also involve aerial antics.

The well-known behaviorist Konrad Lorenz credited the raven as having the "highest mental development" of any species in the bird world. For example, the bird is capable of working alone or in groups to steal food from predator species. One raven may act as a decoy while another grabs the prize. Wild ravens are believed to live as long as 40 years, occasionally even longer.

Black-capped Chickadee *Poecile atricapilla*

DESCRIPTION Adult: Cap and bib black; cheeks white.
SIZE Length to 5¼" (13 cm).
NESTING Nest: In a tree cavity or old woodpecker nest, 5–20' (1.5–6 m) off the ground, or the bird may excavate its own nest cavity. **Eggs:** Normally 6–8, white with reddish brown speckles.
HABITAT Deciduous forests.

This year-round resident is familiar to young and old, and often visits bird feeders. During fall and winter, the black-capped chickadee eats seeds and hides many more. Researchers have determined that the bird grows new brain cells—one cell to remember where it hid each seed. The hippocampus of the brain is used for memory, and new cells replace old ones as they are needed. The black-capped chickadee is known to live as long as 12 years. It is also remarkable for its ability to reduce its body temperature at night by 50–54°F (10–12°C) to save energy.

Red-breasted Nuthatch *Sitta canadensis*

DESCRIPTION Cap black; eyeline black; underparts rufous.
SIZE Length to 4½" (11 cm).
NESTING Nest: Excavated in a tree cavity or in an abandoned woodpecker nest, 5–40' (1.5–12 m) off the ground. Nest materials include grass, moss, bark and feathers. **Eggs:** Normally 5–6, white.
HABITAT Mature coniferous and mixed-wood forests.

The red-breasted nuthatch, a year-round resident, frequents feeders containing sunflower seeds and suet, but it normally finds its food while moving head first down a tree trunk. This is an industrious species, which digs out its own cavities or occupies a disused woodpecker nest. The bird may smear the entrance to its nest cavity with sap to discourage insects such as ants from entering the nesting chamber. Included in the repertoire of songs is the nasal territorial song *yna-yna-yna*.

White-breasted Nuthatch *Sitta carolinensis*

DESCRIPTION Adult: Head with black cap and white face; breast white.
SIZE Length to 5¾" (14.5 cm).
NESTING Nest: In a cavity 15–60' (4.5–18 m) off the ground. **Eggs:** Normally 5–9, white with reddish brown spots.
HABITAT Deciduous and mixed forests.

The female white-breasted nuthatch builds her nest carefully in a natural cavity or abandoned woodpecker's hole. Adults have been observed sweeping the outside and inside of their nest with crushed insects in their bills, an activity that may repel predators. Mud is added occasionally to the rim of the nest, perhaps to reduce the size of the entrance hole so that larger birds, such as European starlings (p. 70), cannot enter the nest chamber. While most cavity-nesting birds lay white eggs, this species' eggs are mottled with various browns. Scientists have no explanation for this.

Brown Creeper *Certhia americana*

DESCRIPTION Upper parts streaked with brown; underparts white.
SIZE Length to 5¼" (13 cm).
NESTING Nest: Behind tree bark or in a tree cavity, 5–15' (1.5–4.5 m) off the ground. Nest materials include twigs, bark, moss and leaves; nest is lined with feathers. **Eggs:** Normally 5–6, white speckled with reddish brown.
HABITAT Mature forests.

The brown creeper searches for insects and spiders by starting low on a tree trunk and working its way up and onto the branches in a spiral pattern. During courtship, the male often chases the female, feeding her as she flutters her wings. The female does all the incubating and brooding of the young, but males help feed the young once they have hatched. If danger threatens, both adults and young hide from predators by pressing their well-camouflaged bodies against the bark of trees. Their song begins with two distinctive notes: *sing! sing!*

House Wren *Troglodytes aedon*

DESCRIPTION Adult: Back and wings dark brown; belly buff; eyebrow faint; tail long.
SIZE Length to 4¾" (12 cm).
NESTING Nest: In any natural or man-made cavity. Nest materials include twigs, grass, animal fur and feathers. **Eggs:** Normally 6–7, white with reddish brown blotches.
HABITAT Open woods, thickets and gardens.

Aptly named, the house wren has a tendency to nest near people's homes, in any available enclosed space such as old woodpecker holes, nest boxes and drainpipes. The male often makes additional dummy nests for the female to choose from. The house sparrow (see p. 87), an introduced species, competes with this native species for nest sites and is believed to be the reason for the decline of the house wren in some areas. The house wren, in turn, is notorious for destroying or removing other birds' eggs. Scientists are uncertain about the reason for this—perhaps they are reducing the competition for food.

Marsh Wren *Cistothorus palustris*

DESCRIPTION Adult: Black triangular patch with white stripes on back; breast white; belly buff; eye line white and prominent.
SIZE Length to 5" (12.5 cm).
NESTING Nest: Attached to cattails, bulrushes or other marsh plants. Nest materials include wet grass, cattails and rushes; nest is lined with grass, plant down and feathers. **Eggs:** Normally 4–5, light brown with dark brown blotches.
HABITAT Cattail or rush marshes.

The marsh wren is a songster, and it favors singing sites that are hidden from view. Rarely does the male venture far from such locations. Its distinctive song has been described as everything from a gurgling rattle to a rattling chatter. To view the marsh wren is often difficult—sometimes seemingly impossible. The patient viewer is most likely to be rewarded: eventually the male climbs to a position where he can be seen. This wren builds distinctive, sphere-shaped covered nests among cattails and rushes. Males have been known to make as many as 20 dummy nests, possibly to impress females, to mark territory or to distract predators from the real nest. Males are also known to be polygynous, mating with as many as 3 females each. This is more likely to occur in areas with abundant insects, the main food of this species.

American Dipper *Cinclus mexicanus*

DESCRIPTION Gray overall with a stocky build.
SIZE Length to 6½" (16 cm).
NESTING Nest: On a rock ledge or among roots on a stream bank, often behind a waterfall. Domed nest is made from mosses, twigs and grass. **Eggs:** Normally 4–5, white.
HABITAT Along clear mountain streams.

The American dipper is capable of walking or swimming along the bottoms of fast-moving streams to obtain food. Meals consist primarily of aquatic insect larvae living under stones, as well as insects flying above the water. The water ouzel, as this bird is sometimes called, raises 2 broods per year in parts of its range. It is a year-round resident that often moves down from higher elevations during the winter months, and its continuous push-ups (bobbing) are characteristic.

Golden-crowned Kinglet *Regulus satrapa*

DESCRIPTION Adult: Upper parts grayish-olive; underparts whitish; wing bars (2) white. **Male:** Crown patch orange. **Female:** Crown patch yellow.
SIZE Length to 4" (10 cm).
NESTING Nest: In a conifer 6–60' (2–18 m) off the ground. Nest is a deep hanging cup made up of a variety of moss, lichens, bark strips, twigs and leaves. **Eggs:** Normally 8–9, whitish to pale buff.
HABITAT Coniferous forests, and migrates through a variety of forested habitats.

The tiny golden-crowned kinglet is more often heard than seen; in fact, it is one of our smallest birds. It prefers moister closed forests, where it may be found alone, in flocks or in the company of the black-capped chickadee (p. 63), brown creeper (p. 64) and red-breasted nuthatch (p. 63). At the nest, this species lays a large number of eggs that are often stacked in two layers—an excellent arrangement for the efficient incubation of many eggs.

Similar Species: The ruby-crowned kinglet (*Regulus calendula*) has a red patch on its head that is normally concealed unless courtship activities are underway, or the bird is defending its territory. Its distinctive song can be described as a rolling, bubbly warble.

Mountain Bluebird *Sialia currucoides*

DESCRIPTION Male: Head, back and wings sky blue; breast lighter. **Female:** Wings and tail blue; body gray.
SIZE Length to 7¼" (18 cm).
NESTING Nest: In a natural tree cavity or old woodpecker hole. Nest materials include grass, twigs, rootlets, hair and feathers. **Eggs:** Normally 5–6, bluish.
HABITAT Open areas with well-spaced trees.

The mountain bluebird is a quiet, gentle member of the bird world. It is a beautiful species, capable of hovering for several seconds while hunting for large insects. Nesting takes place in the holes of trees, often those made by the northern flicker (see p. 55). These birds also readily accept nest boxes in suitable locations. Thousands of such boxes have been set up along various rural roads throughout North America to attract bluebirds, and these bluebird trails have been very successful in attracting tree swallows (p. 58) as well. European starlings (p. 70) and house sparrows (p. 87), however, often take over potential nest sites for this species.

Similar Species: The western bluebird (*Sialia mexicana*) is a similar species, easily distinguishable by its orange breast.

Hermit Thrush *Catharus guttatus*

DESCRIPTION Adult: Back and wings brown; rump and tail reddish brown.
SIZE Length to 7" (18 cm).
NESTING Nest: On the ground or in a tree, 3–12' (1–3.5 m) off the ground. Nest materials include twigs, moss, weeds, bark, pine needles and rootlets. **Eggs:** Normally 4, bluish, occasionally with brown speckles.
HABITAT Forested areas.

The hermit thrush is well known for its fabulous flute-like song, a series of notes that start at a low pitch and then rise. This song is symbolic of forest life of North America, and considered by some to be the finest bird-song on the continent. The hermit thrush inhabits higher elevations. It is known for its habit of occasionally flicking its tail upward, then slowly lowering it.

Similar Species: The Swainson's thrush (*Catharus ustulatus*) is a late migrant that occupies lower elevations and is often found in wetland environments and forest margins. It lacks the reddish brown rump and tail of the hermit thrush.

American Robin *Turdus migratorius*

DESCRIPTION Back and wings gray-brown; breast brick red. **Male:** Head black.
SIZE Length to 10" (25 cm).
NESTING Nest: In a tree, 5–25' (1.5–8 m) off the ground. Nest materials include grass, twigs and mud.
Eggs: Normally 4, light blue.
HABITAT A wide range of habitats.

For many people, the song of the American robin marks the arrival of spring. This amazing species has adapted well to human environments and often has 2 clutches in one year. It feeds on earthworms, cutworms and many other insects, thriving where many other thrushes have not. In the fall, however, its diet changes considerably to a selection of berries and other fruits. The American robin is a common resident throughout North America. Sometimes individuals are caught in snowstorms and cannot obtain food. At such times they will eat pieces of apple from a feeder, placed there by people wishing to help them out.

Gray Catbird *Dumetella carolinensis*

DESCRIPTION Adult: Overall dark gray; head with a black cap.
SIZE Length to 8½" (22 cm).
NESTING Nest: In dense shrubbery or thicket, 3–10' (1–3 m) off the ground. **Eggs:** Normally 3–4, greenish blue.
HABITAT Forest edges, brush, shrubby areas and similar environments.

The gray catbird is well known for its ability to mimic a wide variety of birds, as well as "rusty hinge" sounds. It is especially famous for its mewing cat-like call, hence its common name.
   The varied diet of this bird includes such natural items as insects during the summer and berries in the fall. Catbirds are also known to eat various items from feeders, including peanuts, peanut butter, chopped fresh fruit, suet, cooked potatoes and raisins. Some individuals are even known to have dined on a breakfast of cornflakes and milk.

Cedar Waxwing *Bombycilla cedrorum*

DESCRIPTION Brown overall; head with crest; wings gray with red (waxy) spots; tail with yellow (waxy) tip; undertail coverts white; belly yellowish.
SIZE Length to 7¼" (18 cm).
NESTING Nest: In a tree, 6–20' (1.5–6 m) off the ground. Nest materials include twigs, grass, moss and hair. **Eggs:** Normally 3–5, gray with brown spots.
HABITAT Open areas where berries are available.

The cedar waxwing, one of only 3 species of waxwings worldwide, delights in dining primarily on seasonal fruits. Waxwings are frugivores (fruit eaters), enjoying raspberry, rose, bearberry and juniper, among other fruits. These berries contribute the carotenoid pigments the birds need to produce the wax-like secretions on their wings and tail tips.

Similar Species: The Bohemian waxwing (*Bombycilla garrulus*) is similar in coloration. This winter visitor is a larger bird, with white bars and yellow spots on the wings and cinnamon undertail coverts.

Loggerhead Shrike *Lanius ludovicianus*

DESCRIPTION Adult: Back bluish gray; head bluish gray with a black mask; underparts white; bill with a small hook. **Juvenile:** Paler overall with light areas barred.
SIZE Length to 9" (23 cm).
NESTING Nest: In a tree or shrub, 5–30' (1.5–9 m) off the ground.
Eggs: Normally 5–6, grayish white to pale buff with brown and gray spots.
HABITAT Semi-open areas, with trees and shrubs serving as lookout posts.

The loggerhead shrike is a hunter, well known for its habit of killing prey and storing it on thorns or in the forks of twigs. This species feeds primarily on insects, but when insects are scarce, small birds and mammals such as mice are taken. During courtship, the size of the male's larder and his ability to provide food may be a factor in his acceptance by a mate.

Similar Species: The northern shrike (*Lanius excubitor*) is larger with a paler back and head, as well as lightly barred underparts, and its bill has a slightly larger hook.

69

European Starling *Sturnus vulgaris*

DESCRIPTION Adult: Overall black with white spots (feathers are tipped with white). **Breeding adult:** Body iridescent overall, bill yellow.
SIZE Length to 8½" (21 cm).
NESTING Nest: In a cavity. Nest materials include twigs, grass, leaves and feathers.
Eggs: Normally 4–6, greenish white or bluish white.
HABITAT Farmlands, fields and similar situations; urban settings.

The European starling was introduced to North America over a century ago and is now so common throughout most of the continent that it is regarded as a pest. It is a social species, whose flocks number in the thousands during the winter months. Starlings are aggressive, occupying nesting cavities that would otherwise be used by several native species, and occasionally laying their eggs in the nests of other birds. They are also well known for their ability to mimic the songs and calls of other birds.

Red-eyed Vireo *Vireo olivaceus*

DESCRIPTION Adult: Crown blue-gray; eyebrow white with black edge above and below; eyes ruby red.
SIZE Length to 6" (15 cm).
NESTING Nest: In a tree, 5–30' (1.5–9 m) off the ground. **Eggs:** Normally 4, white with brown or black spots.
HABITAT Deciduous and mixed wood forests.

Each spring the male arrives early, with its crystal clear song, to proclaim its territory. As part of the courtship, the male feeds the female choice foods prior to nest building. The female is a meticulous housekeeper, taking great care to keep the nest in fine shape throughout the nesting period, adding and repositioning materials as needed. The task of feeding the young falls to the female approximately 75 percent of the time, and to the male for the remaining 25 percent. Occasionally two nests are made during a single season. The red-eyed vireo is the prime victim of the parasitic habits of the brown-headed cowbird (p. 82).

Similar Species: The warbling vireo (*Vireo gilvus*) is a rather plain looking species, gray above with white underparts and a white eyebrow that has no dark upper border. It can be found in open deciduous woods.

Yellow Warbler *Dendroica petechia*

DESCRIPTION Male: Body yellow; underside streaked with red; eye dark. **Female:** Body yellow; eye dark.
SIZE Length to 5" (12.5 cm).
NESTING Nest: In a tree or shrub, 2–60' (.5–18 m) off the ground. Nest materials include grass and shredded bark; nest is lined with plant down. **Eggs:** Normally 4–5, whitish with brown and gray speckles.
HABITAT Deciduous trees or shrubs.

The brilliant colors of the yellow warbler inspire all who see this bird, and its vibrant song is not soon forgotten. It is a lively song, sometimes described as *sweet-sweet-sweet summer swee*—but it certainly loses something in the translation.

Female yellow warbler.

This species is sometimes parasitized by the brown-headed cowbird (see p. 82). When a nest is parasitized, the yellow warbler either deserts the nest or builds a new nest over the old one. One nest contained a total of 6 nests, 5 of which contained cowbird eggs. In some areas of North America, as many as 75% of warblers' nests have been parasitized.

Similar Species: The orange-crowned warbler (*Vermivora celata*) is a common warbler that is often found in shrubby areas. It is olive above and lighter below with streaks on the breast. Its orange crown is not often seen in the field.

71

Tennessee Warbler *Vermivora peregrina*

DESCRIPTION Breeding male: Upper parts green; crown gray; eyebrow white. **Female:** Overall tinged with yellow or olive. **Male in fall:** Overall breeding plumage tinged with more yellow than that of the female.
SIZE Length to 4¾" (12 cm).
NESTING Nest: In a depression on the ground, under shrubs or tall grass. **Eggs:** Normally 5–6, white with brown or purple markings.
HABITAT Deciduous and mixed wood forests in which poplars predominate.

The fine voice of the Tennessee warbler is an excellent aid in identifying this species, as it sings its distinctive *ten-ten-ten-ten-tenna-tenna-tenna-tenna-seeseeseeseeseesee*.

The common name of this warbler originates from the location where it was first discovered, Cumberland River, Tennessee. This bird is not a resident there but merely migrates through on its way north. It is commonly seen during its migration from its winter range in the tropical regions of South America to its summer breeding range across Canada.

Yellow-rumped Warbler *Dendroica coronata*

DESCRIPTION Male: Back, wings and head blue; rump, throat and cap yellow. **Female:** Overall duller in color than the male.
SIZE Length to 5½" (14 cm).
NESTING Nest: In a tree, 4–50' (1–15 m) off the ground. Nest materials include bark, twigs and roots; nest is lined with hair and feathers. **Eggs:** Normally 4–5, cream-colored with brown and gray speckles.
HABITAT Treed areas.

The yellow-rumped warbler is a fine-dining insectivore, enjoying ants, wasps, house flies, crane flies, gnats, true bugs and other insects. This very early migrant is also known to feed on some vegetation. In springtime, migrants announce their arrival from their winter homes in South America. Their beautiful and distinctive warble has been described as *seet-seet-seet-seet trrrrr*. These warblers often accompany other species while on migration.

The yellow-rumped warbler can be separated into two forms or subspecies, the "Audubon's warbler" and "myrtle warbler," which were once considered separate species. Breeding males of both species have distinctive plumage. The adult male "Audubon's warble" displays bright patches of yellow on the crown, throat, side and rump. The adult male "myrtle warbler" displays bright patches of yellow on the crown, side and rump, but has a white throat and eyebrow. Both subspecies can be observed in the west.

Common Yellowthroat *Geothlypis trichas*

DESCRIPTION Male: Mask black with white border; throat and breast bright yellow; upper parts olive green. **Female:** Face does not have mask; throat and breast yellow; upper parts olive green.
SIZE Length to 5" (12.5 cm).
NESTING Nest: Near the ground on weeds, grasses and shrubs. Nest materials include weeds, grass, sedges, leaves and bark; nest is lined with grass and hair. **Eggs:** Normally 3–5, whitish with brown and black speckles.
HABITAT Wetlands, including marshes, swamps and bogs, as well as willow and alder thickets.

A visit to a cattail marsh is not complete until the distinctive voice of the common yellowthroat is heard. Its voice is often described as *whitchity, whitchity, whitchity*, or occasionally as *your money, your money, your money*. Its call sounds like a rubber band— *doink*. The common yellowthroat also has a flight song in which the male begins singing on a low shrub, then flies to a height of 25–100' (8–30 m) in an undulating pattern, from which it swoops down to a new low perch. The song and various notes are only made on the bird's ascent and at the peak of its display; the descent takes place without calls or song. Males are normally monogamous but in at least one instance a male is known to have had two mates. Brown-headed cowbirds (see p. 82) often deposit their eggs in the nests of this host.

Wilson's Warbler *Wilsonia pusilla*

DESCRIPTION Back and wings olive; underparts yellow. **Male:** Cap black; face yellow. **Female:** Cap sometimes blackish; forehead yellowish.
SIZE Length to 4¾" (12 cm).
NESTING Nest: On the ground or in a shrub or vine, to 3' (1 m) off the ground. Nest materials include leaves, grass and moss; nest is lined with grass and hair. **Eggs:** Normally 4–6, cream-colored with brown markings.
HABITAT Moist woods, bogs and thickets.

The Wilson's warbler is a very active species with a habit of twitching its wings and tail while perched. It is a delightful wood warbler and common in moist areas, where it actively pursues a great variety of insects with aerial acrobatics. This bird's song is loud and has been written as *chi chi chi chi chet chet*. Biologists have discovered that populations breeding as far north as Alaska winter in the southern portion of the wintering range, Central America. However, southern breeding populations, such as those in California, winter only as far south as Baja California. It is unknown why this pattern of migration, called leapfrog migration, occurs.

Western Tanager *Piranga ludoviciana*

DESCRIPTION Breeding male: Belly yellow; face red; back black. **Female:** Back gray; head greenish yellow; underparts greenish yellow or gray.
SIZE Length to 7" (18 cm).
NESTING Nest: In a tree, 15–65' (4.5–20 m) off the ground. Nest is made from twigs, grass and rootlets, and is lined with hair. **Eggs:** Normally 3–5, bluish with brown blotches.
HABITAT Conifer forests in summer.

Although the western tanager is a mountain resident, it is often observed in a wide range of other habitats while migrating to its summer residence. The stunning plumage of this bird is memorable. This tanager may also visit feeders to eat fresh fruit, including halved oranges. While nesting, males are often heard singing their robin-like song from a high perch in the forest canopy. The call is distinctive, a quick *prid-a-dit*. The brown-headed cowbird (see p. 82) is known to parasitize the nests of the western tanager with its eggs.

Rose-breasted Grosbeak *Pheucticus ludovicianus*

DESCRIPTION Breeding adult: Head and back black; breast rose red; wing bars white; bill large and triangular.
SIZE Length to 8" (20 cm).
NESTING Nest: In tree or shrub, 3–25' (1–8 m) off the ground. **Eggs:** Normally 3–5, greenish blue with reddish brown spots.
HABITAT Deciduous and mixed wood forests.

The song of the rose-breasted grosbeak strongly resembles that of the American robin, but this bird's song phrases run together in a continuous series, without breaks. Unlike other species, this one is not secretive at the nest site, and males are actually known to sing as they sit on the eggs in the nest. Both sexes build the nest and incubate the eggs, in a nest so flimsy that the eggs can often be seen from underneath the nest. Biologists have determined that populations of this species have declined by a third since 1980.

Spotted Towhee *Pipilo maculatus*

DESCRIPTION Male: Hood black; breast white below with chestnut sides; eyes red. **Female:** Colors subdued.
SIZE Length to 8½" (22 cm).
NESTING Nest: On or near the ground. Nest materials include leaves, bark and grasses. **Eggs:** Normally 2–6, cream-colored with brown blotches.
HABITAT Forest edges and shrubby areas.

The spotted towhee scratches at the ground using both feet at once, to stir up leaves on the ground in search of food. The cheery *chewink* or *chweee* call of this species can often be heard from ground level before the bird is seen. Males can be heard singing with a high trill as they proclaim their territory from tall shrubs. This sparrow-like bird can be found from southern Alberta to central Guatemala. It was formerly called the rufous-sided towhee, along with a similar species, the eastern towhee (*Pipilo erythrophthalmus*), which lacks spots.

Vesper Sparrow *Pooecetes gramineus*

DESCRIPTION Adult: Back barred with brown; ear patch dark; shoulder patch chestnut; outer tail feathers white.
SIZE Length to 6¼" (16 cm).
NESTING Nest: In a tree, 10–19' (3–6 m) off the ground. **Eggs:** Normally 2–4, white to pale greenish white with brown and gray blotches.
HABITAT Prairies, roadsides and some meadows.

The vesper sparrow is primarily an insectivore that also consumes some seeds. It is the only sparrow that regularly sings at twilight with a truly vibrant voice. Its beautiful song has been declared even sweeter than that of the song sparrow (p. 77). The male is also known to sing a flight song during its courtship display. One study identified the main predators of this sparrow as skunks, raccoons and cats, both feral and domestic.

Savannah Sparrow *Passerculus sandwichensis*

DESCRIPTION Eyebrow yellow; breast and sides streaked; back and wings dark brown.
SIZE Length to 5½" (14 cm).
NESTING Nest: On the ground, made from grass, lined with fine grass.
Eggs: Normally 2–6, whitish with brown speckles.
HABITAT Open areas, especially grasslands and wetlands.

This widespread resident may be seen and heard singing on top of a shrub or fence post in open country. Here they nest, going largely undetected until the male proclaims his territory. The male's buzzy "song" may be summarized as *tea tea tea teeeeea today*.

The savannah sparrow is a common and widespread species that dines on a variety of foods including seeds, beetles and grasshoppers. Males may have more than one mate, and females have been known to lay eggs in other savannah sparows' nests as well as their own.

Fox Sparrow *Passerella iliaca*

DESCRIPTION Head and back dark brown to dark gray; rump and tail reddish; underparts heavily spotted with a large central blotch; yellow lower bill (mandible).
SIZE Length to 7" (18 cm).
NESTING Nest: On the ground or in a low shrub or tree. Nest is made from grass, weeds and moss, and lined with grass. **Eggs:** Normally 2–5, greenish blotched with reddish brown.
HABITAT Open shrubby and forest areas.

The fox sparrow is often seen scratching its feet along the ground as it forages for seeds, fruits, insects and various other foods. It inhabits elevations from sea level to subalpine heights. The distinctive song of this bird is loud and melodious. Like many songbirds, this sparrow migrates in flocks during the darkness of night.

Similar Species: This common species is easily confused with the song sparrow (p. 77). Both species display spotted underparts and a central breast spot. The fox sparrow is dark overall with a yellow lower mandible and lacks facial markings, while the song sparrow is lighter overall with a gray eyebrow and dark bill.

Song Sparrow *Melospiza melodia*

DESCRIPTION Breast white with dark brown streaks and central spot; eyebrow gray; bill dark.
SIZE Length to 6" (15 cm).
NESTING Nest: On the ground or in a tree or shrub, to 10' (3 m) off the ground. Nest materials include weeds, grass, bark strips; nest is lined with grass, rootlets and hair. **Eggs:** Normally 4, whitish with reddish brown blotches.
HABITAT Dense shrubby areas.

The song of the song sparrow is rich and varied, beginning with a *sweet, sweet, sweet* and followed by a trill or warble. It has also been said to sing *hip-hip-hooray boys, spring's here!*—an appropriate phrase, since this sparrow begins its nesting activities early in the spring. This bird's song is so distinctive that it is embedded in both its common name and its scientific name, *melodia* ("singing" or "song").

The song sparrow feeds primarily on seeds and insects, which makes it an important factor in the natural control of weed seeds and injurious insects. Adults may nest more than once during the season, and in fact there is one record of a pair successfully raising 4 broods in one season, the last nest also containing 2 eggs of the brown-headed cowbird (see p. 82).

White-crowned Sparrow *Zonotrichia leucophrys*

DESCRIPTION Crown black-and-white striped; throat gray; wings and back brown.
SIZE Length to 7" (18 cm).
NESTING Nest: On the ground or in low shrubbery. Nest is made from grass, twigs, rootlets and bark, and lined with grass, feathers and hair. **Eggs:** Normally 4–5, whitish to greenish with reddish brown speckles.
HABITAT Dense shrubby areas.

The spring arrival of the white-crowned sparrow is most welcome after the quiet winter months. This species inhabits a wide range of open habitats, from treeline to lakeshore. Here it happily announces its presence with a vibrant, quite variable song that has been written out as *more-wet-wetter-chee-zee* or the undignified *I, I, I gotta go wee-wee now*. The white-crowned sparrow often nests in close proximity to humans in both urban and rural settings, including urban residential backyards, orchards, clearcut areas and farmlands. It feeds on seeds, insects and occasionally fruit and buds.

77

Dark-eyed Junco *Junco hyemalis*

DESCRIPTION "Slate-colored" form male: Back and hood black; breast white; outer tail feathers white. **"Slate-colored" form female:** Colors drab overall.
SIZE Length to 6¼" (16 cm).
NESTING Nest: On the ground. Nest built from grass and leaves, lined with fine grass, hair and feathers. **Eggs:** Normally 3–5, whitish with brown and gray markings.
HABITAT A wide variety of habitats.

The coloration of the dark-eyed junco varies considerably across North America, where several forms (subspecies) occur. The "slate-colored" form is widespread and commonly found throughout most of North America. The "Oregon" form includes a black hood, and in another form the bird's back is gray. This year-round resident is a regular visitor to bird feeders over the winter months. The cheery presence of the dark-eyed junco is always a welcome sight!

Snow Bunting *Plectrophenax nivalis*

DESCRIPTION Breeding adult: Back is black; head and breast white; wings black and white. **Winter:** Back is brown; head with black and brown cap; wings black and white.
SIZE Length to 6¾" (17 cm).
NESTING Nest: In a protected site among rocks, or similar area. **Eggs:** Normally 4–7, white to pale blue-green, marked with black and brown.
HABITAT Prairies, fields, shores and similar areas.

The snow bunting is a wanderer that breeds in the Arctic tundra and makes its way south during the winter. It is often observed flying in flocks, seemingly in a swirling motion, reminiscent of a snowstorm. As a result, these birds are sometimes referred to affectionately as "snowflakes." This distinctive species burrows into the snow to keep warm during cold winter nights when the temperature regularly reaches –40°F (–40°C). Its winter diet consists primarily of seeds.

Western Meadowlark *Sturnella neglecta*

DESCRIPTION Breeding: Back and wings brown; breast yellow with a black V-shaped band; outer tail feathers white.
SIZE Length to 9½" (24 cm).
NESTING Nest: On the ground, in areas of dense grass. Nest is a domed structure with a side entrance. **Eggs:** Normally 3–7, white with brown and purple spots.
HABITAT Grasslands, pastures and similar areas.

This impressive looking songster nests near croplands; so, as with the burrowing owl (p. 47), it has often been poisoned by insecticides applied to agricultural crops. The

male western meadowlark commonly nests with two and occasionally three females simultaneously. His flute-like warbling song is often followed immediately by a rattle-like call emitted by the female. The nest is one of only a few species in North America that is constructed with a dome-like cover.

Yellow-headed Blackbird *Xanthocephalus xanthocephalus*

DESCRIPTION Adult male: Overall black; head and breast bright yellow; wing bar white. **Female:** Overall streaked with brown.
SIZE Length to 9½" (24 cm).
NESTING Nest: On or above water, lashed to cattails, bulrushes or similar vegetation, to 3' (1 m) off the ground. **Eggs:** Normally 4–5, white spotted with brown and purple.
HABITAT Wetlands, prairies and similar areas.

The yellow-headed blackbird is a colony nester with a horrific croaking voice that is unmusical at best. The spectacular courtship display of the male includes bowing toward the female. He may then take up residence with a single female or a harem of several nesting females—typically three or four, and occasionally as many as eight. Females are largely responsible for the raising of the young, with some help from males.

These birds sometimes nest in the same marshes as the red-winged blackbird (p. 80). The yellow-headed blackbird is larger, so it often evicts the red-winged blackbird from a territory in dispute, even though the red-winged blackbird arrived earlier on the breeding grounds.

Red-winged Blackbird *Agelaius phoeniceus*

DESCRIPTION Male:
Body black; shoulder patches red edged with yellow. **Female:** Brown overall; heavily streaked below.
SIZE Length to 8¾" (22 cm).
NESTING Nest: Attached to cattails, bulrushes or willows. Nest materials include grass, reeds and leaves; nest is lined with grasses. **Eggs:** Normally 3–4, greenish with brown blotches.
HABITAT Wetlands.

Male.

The colorful red-winged blackbird has been declared the most abundant land bird in North America, with winter numbers in the United States alone estimated at an astounding 190 million. It is a common and colorful resident, often found in the company of the marsh wren (see p. 65) in spring and summer. The red-winged blackbird is a very vocal species, with a repertoire of many "songs," calls and notes, including *conc-a-ree* or *okalee*, as well as *eat my cheeeses*. Its calls include *chuck* and a metallic *kink*.

Juvenlie.

Brewer's Blackbird *Euphagus cyanocephalus*

DESCRIPTION Male: Overall black; head with purplish gloss; eyes yellow. **Female:** Overall brown; eyes brown.
SIZE Length to 9" (23 cm).
NESTING Nest: On the ground among tall grass, but more often in a tree, 20–40' (6–12 m) off the ground. **Eggs:** Normally 4–6, gray to greenish gray with brown spots.
HABITAT Prairie, fields and similar dry, open areas.

Female.

These blackbirds are colony nesters. They are one of a few species known to often clean each other's feathers, removing lice as they go, a process known as allopreening. To invite another bird to preen, the bird buries its bill in its breast feathers, presenting its fluffed out nape. Female Brewer's blackbirds often present themselves in this way to female red-winged blackbirds, for reasons that remain a mystery.

This is the only blackbird species whose head moves constantly, with a jerking motion, as it walks.

Similar Species: Both sexes of the rusty blackbird (*Euphagus carolinus*) have yellow eyes and lack the iridescent quality of the Brewer's feathers. For habitat, they prefer wet areas to dry ones. The common grackle (*Quiscalus quiscula*) is a glossy black species with a large, keeled black tail.

Brown-headed Cowbird *Molothrus ater*

DESCRIPTION Male: Head dark brown; body metallic black. **Female:** Overall light brown; breast streaked.
SIZE Length to 7½" (19 cm).
NESTING Nest: None; eggs are laid in other species' nests. **Eggs:** Have been known to lay 70 or more in one season, whitish with brown blotches.
HABITAT Rangeland, clearcuts, forest edges and other open habitats.

This common species lays its eggs in the nests of other birds. It has developed several adaptations that make it an effective parasite. The female can lay an egg in a host's nest in less than one minute, while a non-parasitic species requires 21 to 104 minutes. As well, the female cowbird lays an average of 40 eggs during one breeding season, while most perching birds lay 4-6 per clutch. Cowbirds' eggs also require less time to hatch than most species. Not all hosts accept this intruder's egg, however. Among the many responses are to eject the egg outright, to abandon the nest altogether or to construct a new nest over the parasitized one. The brown-headed cowbird is known to parasitize 226 species of birds in North America.

Cowbirds are often found near bison and cattle.

Baltimore Oriole *Icterus galbula*

DESCRIPTION Breeding male:
Head and upper back black; underparts and rump bright orange.
Female: Head and back brownish
olive; underparts dull orange.
SIZE Length to 8¾" (22 cm).
NESTING Nest: Placed in a deciduous tree, 20–30' (6–9 m) off the
ground. Nest is made from string,
fine grass, strips of bark and plant
fibers, and is lined with plant
down and fine grass. **Eggs:**
Normally 4–5, bluish-white with
brown and black markings.
HABITAT Prairie, open grasslands
and similar areas.

The nest of the Baltimore oriole is an intricately woven hanging structure that is strung
from a forked branch. It has a deep pouch, ensuring that the eggs do not get jostled
about even in the highest of winds. This bird takes advantage of infestations of the forest tent caterpillar (*Malacosoma disstria*), feeding on these caterpillars at all stages of
their life cycle. This is an important food source—a single infestation can consist of
millions of insects.

Red Crossbill *Loxia curvirostra*

DESCRIPTION Bill crossed at the
tip. **Male:** Wings dark brown;
overall red. **Female:** Upper parts
brown; underparts yellowish olive.
SIZE Length to 6¼" (16 cm).
NESTING Nest: In a conifer, usually 10–40' (3–12 m) off the
ground. **Eggs:** Normally 3–4,
greenish white or bluish white
with brown and purple spots.
HABITAT Coniferous forests, especially lodgepole pine.

Crossbills are true nomads. They
feed on the seeds of conifers by
extracting them from the cones, an activity for which their crossed bills are specifically
modified. The bird holds down the cone with its mandible while lifting out the seed with
its tongue. The mandible may be crossed to the right or to the left, neither way having
an advantage over the other. Red crossbills are known to begin nesting at any time of
the year if the seed crop is a good one.

Similar Species: The white-winged crossbill (*Loxia leucoptera*) is very similar, except it
has white wing bars and prefers spruce and fir forests.

Evening Grosbeak *Coccothraustes vespertinus*

DESCRIPTION Male: Belly and rump yellow; head dark with yellow eyebrow; wings black and white; bill massive. **Female:** Tan overall; wings black with white patches.
SIZE Length to 8" (20 cm).
NESTING Nest: In a tree, 10–100' (3–30 m) off the ground. Nest is made from twigs, and lined with grasses, moss and pine needles.
Eggs: Normally 3–4, bluish with brown blotches.
HABITAT Mixed and coniferous woods.

The striking colors of the evening grosbeak often cause a great commotion when the birds are viewed for the first time at a feeder. These birds' insatiable appetite for sunflower seeds in winter is truly remarkable. They also feed on the fruit of saskatoon, chokecherry and pin cherry in season, removing the "useless" pulp to get at the seeds inside. This bird can apply a pressure of 110 lbs (50 kg) with its powerful bill to crack the shells of its food. It is a year-round resident that breeds in mixed woods, and often at higher elevations in the mountains as well. Populations of evening grosbeak fluctuate greatly from year to year.

Gray-crowned Rosy-finch *Leucosticte tephrocotis*

DESCRIPTION Male: Dark brown overall; wings and flanks pinkish brown; back of head gray. **Female:** Dark brown overall; back of head gray.
SIZE Length to 6" (15 cm).
NESTING Nest: Among boulders. Nest materials include grass, rootlets, lichens and moss; nest is lined with grass, feathers and hair. **Eggs:** Normally 4–5, white with reddish brown speckles.
HABITAT Rocky alpine areas.

The gray-crowned rosy-finch is a summer resident of the high alpine, and is observed in the company of the white-tailed ptarmigan (see p. 32). It feeds on seeds, berries and insects tucked away in the sparse vegetation. Because it nests in crevices on rock cliffs, this species encounters little competition in its chosen habitat. While on migration, individuals have been observed from sea level and alpine elevations. They accumulate in large flocks while migrating. These flocks have been documented to number from several hundred to 3,000 individuals.

Pine Grosbeak *Pinicola enucleator*

DESCRIPTION Male: Gray overall; head, back and underparts tipped with pink. **Female and juvenile:** Gray overall; head, rump and underparts orange.
SIZE Length to 9" (23 cm).
NESTING Nest: In a conifer, 5–15' (1.5–4.5 m) off the ground. Nest materials include twigs and rootlets; nest is lined with grasses, lichens and moss. **Eggs:** Normally 2–5, green with brown, purple and black speckles.
HABITAT Open coniferous woods.

The pine grosbeak is a colorful resident throughout much of the north. It appears in abundance in some years and not at all in others, perhaps because of variations in weather or food supply. Its diet includes various fruits and the seeds of various conifers, and it is occasionally seen at feeding stations. These birds are seed-lovers, especially fond of sunflower seeds—in fact, their presence is often associated with

abundant seed crops. They nest in subalpine forests, but only a few nests have ever been found. During the winter, the birds move to lower elevations.

Male.

85

Common Redpoll *Carduelis flammea*

DESCRIPTION Breeding male:
Brown with prominent streaking;
breast and forehead rose-colored.
Female: Similar to male, but the
breast lacks the rosy color.
SIZE Length to 5¼" (13 cm).
NESTING Nest: In low shrubs, near
the ground. Nest materials include
fine twigs, grass and moss; nest is
lined with feathers. **Eggs:** Normally
4–5, pale green to bluish green.
HABITAT Birch trees, shrubby and
weedy areas.

"Nomadic" best describes the life of
the common redpoll. Flocks are often
observed during the winter, feeding
in seed trees, especially birch trees.

They will also stop and eat at a feeder if sunflower and niger (thistle) seeds are available. This is a hardy species that moves south from its Arctic summer range each year, but numbers and ranges fluctuate greatly from year to year. Some years they seem to be everywhere; other years they are rarely observed. Food supplies, temperature and snow do not seem to be factors in its populations.

Pine Siskin *Carduelis pinus*

DESCRIPTION Brown with prominent
streaking; base of tail and wing bar
yellow (often only visible in flight).
SIZE Length to 5" (13 cm).
NESTING Nest: In a tree, 10–40' (3-
12 m) off the ground. Nest is made
with twigs, grass and bark strips, and
lined with moss. **Eggs:** Normally 3–4,
bluish with black and brown speckles.
HABITAT Coniferous, deciduous or
shrubby areas.

Pine siskins are common, social birds
that are usually observed randomly in
small flocks in their search for food. They are year-round residents, often attracted to bird feeders, especially if niger (thistle) seeds are at the table. The pine siskin is very fond of seeds from pine, spruce, alder and birch as well as from the catkins of poplars. They nest in loose groups in a sporadic fashion. The female is responsible for all incubation while the male helps to bring food once the young have hatched.

A banded pine siskin was recovered one winter at Revelstoke, B.C., after being banded in New Jersey two years earlier in the summer—2,188 miles (3,500 km) away. This species may be a resident, but it is truly a wanderer as well.

American Goldfinch *Carduelis tristis*

DESCRIPTION **Summer male:** Body yellow; cap and tail black; wings black with white bars. Summer female: Body yellowish brown; wings black. **Winter male:** Body yellowish brown; head yellowish. **Winter female:** Body yellowish brown; wings black.
SIZE Length to 5" (12.5 cm).
NESTING **Nest:** In a tree or shrub. Nest is compact and well made from plant fibers, spider webs and plant down. **Eggs:** Normally 4–6, bluish white, occasionally with brown speckles.
HABITAT Weedy areas and open spaces.

The American goldfinch is primarily a seed eater, favoring the seeds of thistle, dandelion and similar plants. It is a striking species, which also feeds on insects during the summer and dines on smaller seeds at feeders. During the courtship display, the male conducts an exaggerated loop flight while singing his *perchicoree* call. The brown-headed cowbird (see p. 82), which lays its eggs in the nests of many other birds, is discouraged by the American goldfinch. Its grain diet has been found to retard the growth of young cowbirds, causing them to be unable to fledge.

House Sparrow *Passer domesticus*

Male.

DESCRIPTION **Breeding male:** Crown gray; nape chestnut; bib black. **Female:** Back streaked; eye-stripe buff.
SIZE Length to 6¼" (15.5 cm).
NESTING **Nest:** In a cavity, in the nest of other birds. Nest materials include grass, weeds and twigs; nest is lined with feathers. **Eggs:** Normally 3–6, whitish with brown and gray blotches.
HABITAT Farms, towns and cities.

The house sparrow, or English sparrow as it is often called, is an introduced member of the weaver finch family that is now common throughout most of North America. It finds an occupied cavity to nest in, then removes the eggs and evicts and kills the young and adults of the resident species. The house sparrow dines on a wide range of foods, including insects, spiders, small fruit, weed seeds, grain and crumbs, and it frequents bird feeders as well. Over the past few years, this species has declined in numbers, due to a reduction in available nest sites.

Glossary

accipiter: a forest hawk belonging to the genus *Accipiter*.

altricial: referring to hatching that occurs at an early stage of the chick's development.

buteo: a hawk belonging to the genus *Buteo*.

conifer: an evergreen tree that bears needles.

crepuscular: active before dawn and after dusk.

deciduous: referring to trees that lose their leaves annually.

diurnal: active during daylight hours.

insectivore: feeding on insects.

mandible: lower jaw or bill.

nocturnal: active during darkness.

omnivorous: feeding on both animals and plants.

parasitic: referring to a close relationship in which one species benefits at the expense of another.

polyandry: a mating practice in which a female mates with more than one male, but each male mates with only one female.

polygyny: a mating practice in which one male mates with more than one female, but each female mates with only one male.

precocial: referring to hatching that occurs at a late stage of the chick's development.

primary feathers: the elongated feathers on the last segment of the wing.

riparian: pertaining to or along the edge of a river or stream.

scapular: referring to the shoulder area.

speculum: trailing edge of secondary feathers.

Further Reading

BIRDS

Dunne, Pete, Sibley, D. & Sutton, C. 1988. *Hawks in Flight: The Flight Identification of North American Migrant Raptors*. Houghton Mifflin Company. Boston, MA.

Fisher, Chris & John Acorn. 1998. *Birds of Alberta*. Lone Pine Publishing, Edmonton, AB.

Johnsgard, Paul A. 1988. *North American Owls: Biology and Natural History*. Smithsonian Institution Press, Washington, DC.

Kaufman, Kenn. 1996. *Lives of North American Birds*. Houghton Mifflin Co. Boston,MA.

Ritchison, Gary. 1999. *Wild Bird Guides: Downy Woodpecker*. Stackpole Books, Mechanicsburg, PA.

Salt, W. Ray & Jim R. Salt. 1976. *The Birds of Alberta*. Hurtig Publishers, Edmonton, AB.

FEEDERS, BIRDHOUSES & ATTRACTING BIRDS

Boring, John Kadel, et al. 1995. *Natural Gardening: The Nature Company Guide*. The Nature Company & Time Life Books, New York, NY.

Gerhards, Paul. 1999. Birdhouses & Feeders You Can Make: *Complete Plans and Instructions for Bird-Friendly Nesting and Feeding Sites*. Stackpole Books, Mechanicsburg, PA.

Laubach, R. & C. M. Laubach, 1998. *Backyard Birdhouse Book: Building Nestboxes and Creating Natural Habitats*. Story Books, Pownal, VT.

McNeil, Don. 2002. *The Original Birdhouse Book*. Birdwatchers Digest Press, Marietta, OH.

Merilees, Bill. 2000. *The New Gardening For Wildlife: A Guide for Nature Lovers*. Whitecap Books, Vancouver, BC

Troops, Connie. 1994. *Bluebirds Forever*. Voyageur Press, Inc. Stillwater, MN.

Acknowledgments

I would like to thank the many people who assisted with this project.

Mary Schendlinger for her careful editing.

Kevin MacPherson for his insightful scientific editing.

Jim Salt, who generously aided me in photographing birds and locating species for photography.

The staff at various national, provincial and state parks who helped locate species for photography.

The skilled photographers who provided photos. Their names appear below.

Photo Credits

All photos by Duane Sept except the following:

Tony Beck 13B, 14T, 45B, 48B, 50B, 59TL, 64B, 78B

Ed Debois 24B, 27T, 54T, 64T, 76T, 81T, 83T

Ron Erwin 27B, 36T, 72B, 82T, 87T

John Lowman 48T, 74T

Robert McCaw 5BL, 11B, 12T, 13T, 14B, 21T, 26T, 29B, 30T, 37B, 41T, 44B, 51B, 53T, 53B, 55T, 57T, 57B, 60B, 63B, 66B, 67B, 68B, 70T, 70B, 71T, 71B, 73B, 74B, 78T, 79T, 81B, 83B, 86B

Jim Salt 56T, 61B, 65T

Susan Servos-Sept 96

Cleve Wershler 72T

Index

About the Author

Duane Sept is a biologist, freelance writer and professional photographer. His biological work has included research on various wildlife species and service as a park naturalist. His award-winning photographs have been published internationally, in displays and in books, magazines and other publications, for clients that include BBC Wildlife, Parks Canada, Nature Canada, National Wildlife Federation and World Wildlife Fund.

Today Duane brings a wealth of information to the public as an author, in much the same way he has inspired thousands of visitors to Canada's parks. His published books include *The Beachcomber's Guide to Seashore Life in the Pacific Northwest* (Harbour Publishing) and *Common Wildflowers of British Columbia* (Calypso Publishing). He lives on the Sunshine Coast of British Columbia with his family.